RAYMOND HOOD, ARCHITECT

"His practice was a joy-ride, in which everybody got a thrill, including the client."

—T. E. TALLMADGE

1928

1932

Endpapers: Project for Pawtucket City Hall (drawing by Raymond Hood), *Chicago Tribune* Building (Pen and Ink by Edmund Bateman Morris, F.A.I.A.), *Daily News* Building, New York (Pen and Ink by Edmund Bateman Morris, F.A.I.A.), Rockefeller Center (Pen and Ink by Arthur C. Holden).

RAYMOND HOOD,

ARCHITECT

Form Through Function in the American Skyscraper

by WALTER H. KILHAM, Jr. F.A.I.A.

ARCHITECTURAL BOOK PUBLISHING CO., INC.

NEW YORK

This book endorsed by
The American Institute of Architects

Library of Congress Cataloging in Publication Data

Kilham, Walter Harrington, Jr.,
Raymond Hood, architect.

1. Hood, Raymond Mathewson, 1881–1934.
NA737.H57K54   720′.92′4   73–12395
ISBN 0–8038–0218–8

Published simultaneously in Canada by
Saunders of Toronto, Ltd., Don Mills, Ontario

Printed in the United States of America

TO MY FATHER

CONTENTS

ACKNOWLEDGMENTS

For their guidance and valued criticism throughout
Professor John E. Kouwenhoven
Russell Lynes

For timely facts and helpful details
Trientje Hood Reed
Caroline Hood
Harriet and E. James Gambaro, F.A.I.A.

The New York Chapter of
The American Institute of Architects
whose award to the writer of
The Arnold Brunner Scholarship
made possible the writing of
this book

Acknowledgments

Many others besides those mentioned in the text
contributed their recollections and good suggestions to
the writing of this book, including:

Dale Badgeley
Samuel Chamberlain
Elmer Chase
Francis Christie
Charles Colbert
Ferdinand Eiseman
Brendan Gill
Wallace K. Harrison
Anita Fouilhoux Houston
Earl Lundin
Mrs. Ray Morris
Robert B. O'Connor
Frank Roorda
Gunnar Svalland
Oscar Wiggins

CHAPTER **I**

MEETING RAYMOND HOOD

"No Faith in God"

In the spring of 1927, my last year at the Harvard Architectural School, I was one of a small group selected to make a trip to New York. In talking over what I should see with William Rogers Greeley, a Boston architect, he said that more important than the buildings were the people I should meet, and of these there was no one more outstanding as a moving spirit in architecture than Raymond Hood. A visit to his office was arranged. It was understood that he was too busy to see me personally that day, but I would be welcome to come in and look around.

Upon my arrival I discovered there was a visitor in Hood's private office to whom he was explaining a model he had on his desk. The background was that a Methodist Episcopal parish in Columbus, Ohio had acquired a block of land in the business center, and upon it the congregation wanted to build the greatest church in the world. As the name of Ralph Adams Cram was associated with the design of the finest Gothic cathedrals of the day, the Pastor had been sent to Boston to interview him.

Mr. Cram was delighted to see the Pastor, who explained the plan they had in mind to build this church. However, the congregation was one of businessmen and the site was an extremely valuable one. Therefore, they wished not only to build the greatest church in the world, but to combine it with revenue producing enterprises including a hotel, a YMCA, an apartment house with a swimming pool, and so on. On the street level would be shops to bring in high rentals, and in the basement, the largest garage in Columbus, Ohio. The garage was very important, because, in giving his congregation a place to park their cars on coming to work weekdays the Pastor would indeed make the church the center of their lives.

Mr. Cram was deeply distressed by the idea. He hastened to explain to the Pastor that if it was the congregation's intent to build the "greatest church in the world" it should be a cathedral of solid stone, built to last through the ages to the greater glory of God. It was unthinkable that it be combined with hotels, apartments and retail stores. As for the basement, there would be no room for cars because this noble structure would be constructed on tremendous granite piers, thirty feet across, that would support the structure through all time as a monument to their faith.

The Pastor, though impressed by all this, didn't feel he could return to his building committee and tell them their basement would be full of huge stone piers instead of automobiles. So he came to New York to see Raymond Hood, related the problem and the reaction of Mr. Cram. When he had finished, Mr. Hood said, "The trouble with Mr. Cram is that he has no faith in God. I will design a church for you that will be the greatest church in the world. It will include all the hotels, swimming tanks and candy stores you desire. Furthermore, in the basement will be the largest garage in Christendom because," he continued, "I will build your church on toothpicks and have faith enough in God to believe it will stand up!"

But like many another architect's dream, this one also ended with the model.

"Body and Soul"

By the end of 1927, I had completed my school work and it was time to pick a subject for my final thesis for the Masters degree in Architecture. Although the design curriculum of the school followed the tradition of the Beaux Arts school in Paris where so many American architects had been trained, change was in the air. As a student, I felt we should be looking to America and new ways for our inspiration in architecture, not to Europe and the past. Skyscrapers were American, and a new form of building, but they were clothed in traditional styles. I felt that the new Zoning Law of New York, with its set-back requirements, would break with tradition and a style of American architecture would evolve as a result. The idea for my proposed thesis on this subject was accepted, and in addition, I proposed to

12

"No Faith in God."

Cathedral Project, Columbus, Ohio.

courtesy of McGraw-Hill

work on my own in New York, "where the action was." The new leaders, such men as Harvey Wiley Corbett, Hugh Ferris, and Raymond Hood, were there, and my hope was to get into the office of Raymond Hood. An interim communication lent encouragement.

At the start of the school term in January, 1928, I went down to New York. As soon as the doors opened, I was in the outer office of Raymond Hood and asked to see him. He was busy—I sat there all day—but finally, just before train time, he had a moment. Assuming the purpose of my visit, his first question was what I expected to earn. I replied that money was not my object in coming to his office, but only to work for him. All I would expect was enough to keep body and soul together.

"Well, now," he began, "that is something that interests me very much. I once asked Mr. Cram that question and he said it wasn't worth anything. When I asked Mr. Goodhue he said three dollars. What's 'keeping body and soul together' worth to you?"

I had never earned more than $25.00 a week in my life, but I had been told that they would have small use for you in New York if you mentioned such a sum. So I doubled it and answered, "$50.00 a week."

Hood said he would have to think that over, and changed the subject, asking if I had read *Vers Une Architecture,* by Le Corbusier. By chance I had two of Le Corbusier's books in my bag. Mr. Hood had read only one, so he borrowed the other, *Urbanisme,* to read. Though he did not say anything about hiring me, he did say to come back in the morning.

When I got down to the street, a friend of mine who was waiting for me asked if I had gotten the job. "It doesn't look that way," I replied. "In telling me to come back in the morning I am afraid they want to break it to me gently."

"On the contrary," he said, "I think you have, because you are the first 'Harvard man' he ever asked to come back!"

So it was. In the morning I was put to work on a small job at a somewhat smaller salary. Soon, once I was settled down, I began to come back to the office in the evenings to work on my thesis. One night when I was alone in the drafting room, Mr. Hood came in and asked me what I was doing. I told him about my thesis on skyscrapers and the Zoning Law. Commenting that there was only one way to learn about skyscrapers and that was to work on them, he then said "I am starting one on Forty-Second Street next week, and you can begin it." It was the building for the *New York Daily News.* For me to combine work on my thesis with actual experience was beyond anything I had dreamed possible.

CHAPTER **II**

RAYMOND HOOD, CAPT. PATTERSON AND THE DAILY NEWS

"When You Experts Have Decided"

In 1922, there had been an international competition for the design of the *Chicago Tribune* Building. The winners were John Mead Howells and Raymond M. Hood, and construction of the building followed. Control of the newspaper had been inherited by Col. Robert R. McCormick, leaving his cousin Capt. Joseph Medill Patterson in second place. Interested in the newspaper business, but unwilling to accept a minor role in the affairs of the *Tribune,* Capt. Patterson decided to come to New York and start a paper of his own, a tabloid, the *New York Daily News.* It was a success from the start, and soon his presses were printing enough rolls of newsprint a day to stretch from New York to Florida.

As with his cousin and the *Chicago Tribune,* Capt. Patterson wanted a building for his enterprise in New York. Quoting from the account in their own book, *The News—*

"By the summer of 1927, the need for more space was so urgent that a search for a new building site started in earnest.

"Harry Corash made a center of population study, and found it was in Queens, across the East River from midtown Manhattan. The difficulty of newsprint transport, and the delivery of printed papers made the site impractical at the time; but did suggest 42nd St. as an axis.

Model of zoning envelope (by Walter Kilham, Jr.) for Daily News Building. *model & photo by author*

Plasticene model of scheme below. *courtesy of author*

A concept of the building for the Daily News. Sketch and figures by Raymond Hood

courtesy of Architecture

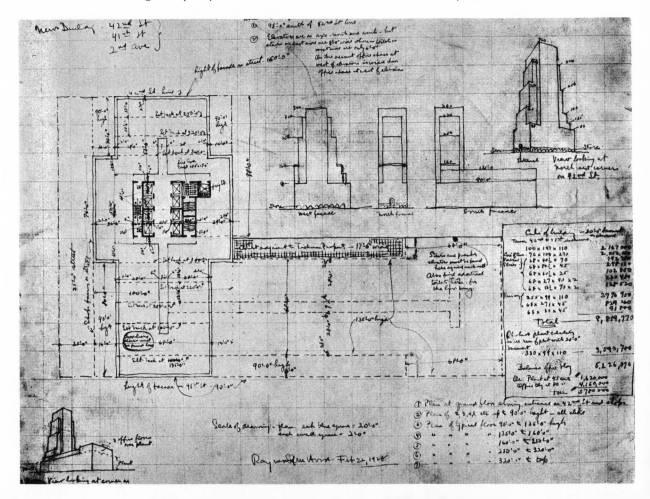

Favorite picture of Joseph Medill Patterson, owner and editor of the *New York Daily News*.
courtesy of N.Y. Daily News

"East of Lexington Ave., the south side of 42nd St. looked like the street across from the railroad station in any small city; a row of old, assorted, unpretentious structures. The real estate firm of Douglas Elliman, Co. was commissioned to acquire a plot in the vicinity. Joseph P. Landauer, over a period of time, succeeded in assembling an L-shaped area.

"The plot had a frontage of 125 feet midblock on 42nd, running through to 41st, and an additional 230 feet on 41st running east to Second Ave. The total cost was something over $2,500,000."

For the design of the building Capt. Patterson selected the same association of architects, Howells and Hood. Raymond Hood was to be the architect in charge of the project and the plans would be done in his office. This was where I came in. I was put to work on the initial sketch plans for the building. I even attended the meetings, a privilege for a beginner. Though still a job of fetch and carry, it gave me a chance to see how things were done at higher levels.

As a building committee for the planning, Capt. Patterson brought together a small group of qualified people that included not only the architect, but also experts in the related fields of construction, real estate, building management, as well as operations of the newspaper itself. At the initial meeting, with things under way, Capt. Patterson withdrew, saying, "When you experts have decided what ought to be done, then I'll come around and see if I will do it."

"Not a Chance"

In making the plans Raymond Hood was not only motivated by a conscientious desire to design the most practical and efficient building he could to meet the requirements of the client, but he was inspired by the contemporary idea of development for the city of the future, and the place of the skyscraper within it. Influenced to some degree by the writings of Le Corbusier in Europe, Raymond Hood visualized a city of towers with wide spaces in between for green parks, broad avenues and esplanades. A practical man, he looked for the gradual achievement of this aim by the acquisition of large sites for buildings on which all the low, obsolete buildings would be torn down but reconstruction, in the form of a tower building, would take place on only a small part of the entire site.

This idea was encouraged to a certain degree by the new Zoning Law, which permitted twenty-five percent of the area to go up as high as it was desired and found practical to build, although it permitted the site to be covered in full up to the setback limit on the street line, the limit being determined by an angle measured from the center of the street. The tower portion of this new building would have light and air all around.

Although the site of the Daily News building ran through the block, it was not large enough to do anything spectacular in the new direction, but it was an opportunity for the architect to try. To Raymond Hood, having an idea was half the battle, but a useless one if not put into effect. To be even the drummer boy in this battle of stimulating contemporary ideas made working for him exciting.

Capt. Patterson had asked for a building for his printing plant, perhaps six stories high, on 41st Street, with some office space on 42nd Street. Usually, such a building would have windows on the street side, but along the property line running between streets, the walls would be blank where they extended above adjacent roofs.

A simple block model of plasticine was made of the printing plant, with an additional lump of clay on one end. If this office space could be higher up, in a tower, it would be better work space, and could have windows if the sides of the tower could be set back from the property line. Any remaining space in the tower not needed by the *News* could be rented at a profit. With all these ideas simmering, the little lump on one end began to grow.

While it was true twenty-five percent of the land area could go to the sky, if the building were carried too high for the size of the lot, the lower floors would be all taken up by elevator shafts. Every conceivable combination of floor plan and number of stories was tried out on paper, to determine the optimum number of floors. The key was in finding the most favorable ratio of usable floor area to the total area as measured around the outside walls. The comparative percentage of return on the investment for each scheme was produced by figuring the capital costs of land, building and its operation against the income value of the space. Successive models were now made in the plasticine of the better schemes, each one with a tower higher than the last.

As the day for the showdown approached, everything was prepared to show Capt. Patterson what he should do. "Remember," said Raymond Hood, "Capt. Patterson is a 'business' man, the stage must be set in a businesslike way. The final scheme must be determined by the figures, the most efficient plan being the one that will net the biggest return on the investment." Nothing was said about what a handsome "tower" it could be, in "a city of the future."

Six or eight schemes were arranged on the conference table, with their calculations, zoning diagrams, and estimates of cost and return. The schemes were illustrated only by the series of block models, instead of perspective renderings. Starting with the basic six stories of the plant through to a height of fifty in a tower, the best return on the investment was indicated by the figures for a building between thirty-five and forty stories high. Capt. Patterson came over. The businesslike presentation didn't fool him a bit. First he looked at the magnificent drawing on the wall that had won the *Chicago Tribune* competition; then he looked at the figures and diagrams. "Well," he said, "I suppose this is one way of doing it," and after a pause, "but what's all this about a tower? I know I run a 'dirty rotten yellow sheet,' but if I can be on a crosstown street to Times Square I'll get my tabloids on the sidewalks in the morning ahead of any of my competitors. All I want is a printing press with a bit of office space attached and here you've got this thing piling up in the air. What's all that for?"

Raymond Hood was all excited. "Capt. Patterson," he said, "do you realize that, with this new Zoning Law, twenty-five percent of your space can go to the sky? Supposing it cost you two hundred thousand dollars a year to run your newspaper, if you build additional space in this tower for rent—making a profit of a hundred thousand dollars a year—it would cut the cost of running your newspaper in half."

"Now wait a minute, wait a minute," said Capt. Patterson, "you want me to do what? Spend five million dollars extra in order to save one hundred thousand dollars a year? Not a chance, Ray, not a chance."

I will never forget the look that came over poor Mr. Hood's face, as the whole effort of months fell into a heap of ashes. Capt. Patterson, however, *19* was never one to let a good man down. After waiting till the effect of his blow was complete, he went over and put his arm around Mr. Hood and said, "Listen, Ray, if you want to build your G— d— tower, go ahead and do it."

And that's how a six story printing press on 41st Street came out to be a thirty-seven story tower building on 42nd.

The Board of Standards and Appeals

With the owner's o.k. to go ahead with the plans for a tower building, one serious problem arose. Although the building was basically a printing plant, the major element of the structure was now an office building: the former would be designed to meet the requirements of the State Labor Law, whereas an office building would come under the New York City Building Code. Unfortunately, the structure was, by definition, one building, and the more restrictive code, in this case the Labor Law, would govern. Applied to an office building, these restrictions would seriously penalize it in a competitive market.

It was true that the two parts of the building would be structurally separated, if for no other reason than that it was desired to keep the vibration of the presses out of the office space, but this did not make it two separate buildings legally. To meet special cases such as this, the law provided a Board of Standards and Appeals to conduct hearings and decide what could be done under the circumstances. For its case the *Daily News* retained the best of lawyers, for we were proceeding with the plans as if the two codes would apply to their respective parts of the building. To try to make the "tower" plan conform to the code for a factory would be an architectural disaster.

As the day of the hearings approached, excitement mounted; all concerned were down in the hearing room as the proceedings began, with the Owner identified as "a domestic corporation in the city of New York, etc. etc." While this part of the proceedings was going on the Chairman at his high desk was observed reading a newspaper—the *Daily News*. Turning to the back page, he held the paper so that everyone present could read the headline of the day: BOARD OF STANDARDS AND APPEALS TO BE INVESTIGATED.

The proceedings began, and as quickly terminated:

"You have filed your application on the green forms requesting a variance from the Labor Law of the State of New York?"

"Yes sir."

"You should have filed your application on the yellow forms for a modification of a decision of the Superintendent of Buildings for the Building Code of the City of New York. The hearings are suspended until your application is received on the proper form. You may request your next turn on the calendar."

This meant six weeks at the least. In the interim, shadowed with uncertainty, work on the plans would continue.

As far as anybody knew, it didn't make a whisper of difference whether an appeal was made from a decision on the Labor Law or the Building Code in order to have a hearing in the first place. But there was a whisper of difference in what might that day be in the headlines of the tabloid *Daily News*.

In the drafting room we were not concerned with the subsequent legal proceedings, and in due course word sifted down that the case had been settled favorably: one part of the structure meeting the requirements of an office building, the other a factory.

"Children Should Be Seen"

Under the Zoning Law the height of a building on the street front was limited. Above this more stories could be added provided the set back from the street came within a certain angle measured from the center of the street. When the area of the plan was reduced within the setback line to twenty-five percent of the lot size, the building could go straight up without further limitations. Speculative builders found these limitations reduced the volume of building they could crowd on a lot compared to the pre-zoning law days, and they used every device they could think of to squeeze more space within the "envelope," as a graphic diagram of the regulation was called. The result was that poorly lighted space, far back from the window, was often constructed, even though the rental for it would be lower.

To Raymond Hood this seemed poor economy. He felt only as much space should be built within the envelope as would receive good light and good rental. There was nothing gained by squeezing in every inch the law would allow; it cost just as much to build the poor space as the good, and it did not bring enough in rent to pay the cost of building it. On this theory the face of the tower, not the wall on the street, would determine the front line of the building. Since most of the office type space requiring adequate light and air would be in the tower, it was important the plan of the tower be most efficient, as it would be repeated on many floors. A distance of about twenty-seven feet back from the window to the elevator lobby or corridor was considered the limit on good office space. Due to the setback law the face of the tower would be at some distance back from the street front, but below the set-back line, any space built between the tower line and the street would only result in deep, uneconomic space.

For this reason Raymond Hood proposed to carry the face of the tower down to the third floor, instead of stopping at the ninth and filling out the lower stories to the street line. Needless to say, Hood's idea would add six stories to the apparent height of the tower. The height of three stories at ground level was required to give a good entrance from the street and provide for a dramatic lobby inside with its high ceiling. The proportions of the base element for the tower that would result seemed very good to everyone. Hood proposed a facade of granite with pierced openings in a decorative design giving daylight into the lobby—it would give importance to the three-story base as the entrance to the building on 42nd Street. The results would have been dramatic, but when the estimates came in for the cost of cutting such a design in granite, it was dropped. The decoration would have to be incised in the polished surface of the stone.

Captain Patterson contributed the following inscription to the decorative panel: "He made so many of them," implying "God loved the common people"—the readers of his tabloid. This was not quite the saying attributed to Abraham Lincoln. According to Bartlett, Lincoln's actual words were, ". . . the Lord prefers common-looking people. That is the reason he makes so many of them." But who would know—Capt. Patterson was also an authority on Lincoln and may have found another source.

With everything resolved about the design of the entrance facade, the final results looked very well on the model. Then, without warning, the *Daily News* concluded that deep space or not, the area available between the tower and the street, all nine stories, would be useful for its operations. No amount of pleading on the part of Raymond Hood did any good. The space was added to the plans, and the great architectural effect of the tower soaring up from the low base was lost.

The *Chicago Tribune* building had been faced with limestone, and Raymond Hood was anxious that the new building be also faced with limestone. But while extra tower floors could be paid for by collecting the rents, nobody would pay extra rent for a limestone facing instead of something cheaper. And so the Captain said, "Make it brick."

I don't want to give the impression that Raymond Hood was losing out in the battles for his ideas. One day he got a tip-off from someone on the staff of the *Daily News* that Capt. Patterson would be over for a meeting. And he would bring up a new idea for the building. This was all right in itself except that, they said, this time it was a really bad idea.

The Captain arrived after lunch, and Raymond Hood took me with him into the meeting in the library. Before the client could open his mouth, Hood announced, "By the way, Capt. Patterson, before we get started, Kilham here has just had a bright idea for the building."

22   This was all news to me. Then Hood went on to explain the new idea,

which would have meant major changes in the appearance of the building. When he finished his presentation he said, "Captain Patterson, do you know what I think of Kilham's idea? I'll tell you—it's lousy; it stinks."

I kept quiet. By now there was no doubt about whose idea it was. As for Capt. Patterson, he didn't say anything either and they went on to other matters.

"The Carving Knife"

René Chambellan was the great architectural sculptor of the day. Mr. Hood enjoyed having him come up to the office with his modeling tools to work on the plasticine block-model of the building. Under his direction, Chambellan would cut off a little here, add a little there, until it seemed to have the right effect—all in coordination with the plans, of course.

Economics had determined the height of the building at thirty-seven stories, and to complete the design it needed a suitable top. Left to itself the roof of the *Daily News* would be a jumble of water tanks, elevator penthouses and vent shafts. On important buildings it was customary to design some elaborate structure of pinnacles, minarets, spires or other classic devices to provide a "silhouette" and hide these homely features. Raymond Hood's solution was simpler—to carry up the outside walls about three more stories, screening all the roof structures from view. Many more buildings were to follow the same idea.

Dominating the mass of the building as an uncompromising shaft, the profile of the tower remained. It conformed to our latest tower plan and was in accordance with the Zoning Law, totaling twenty-five percent of the area of the lot. The shaft may have represented the best solution of the various problems of real estate, economics and zoning involved, but somehow its lines were not aesthetically satisfying to Mr. Hood.

One afternoon, I came into his office where the model was sitting on the corner of the table. Hood commonly left the actual work of modeling to others, but there he was, with a new tool in his hands—a carving knife. "Do you mind," he said, "if I do a little zoning myself?" Whereupon he began slicing pieces of the tower—cutting in steps or set-backs to give a new silhouette. I could hardly believe my eyes. After all that had been said of the value of rental space in the tower, this chiseling was throwing away pure gold.

We backed off to take a look. Somehow, arbitrary or not, the building now had a tapering effect: it began to look the way a modern skyscraper should in the new day of set-backs and towers—nothing that could be explained with a slide rule or a diagram. The scheme, as architects say, had "arrived."

"Two More Mistakes"

As each little decision was made, and each conclusion reached, it was snatched by the drafting room to weave into the fabric of the plans. The "working drawings," a formidable pile, were finally complete. The contract had been negotiated with Hegeman-Harris Co. and there remained only the signing of the contract document before the steam shovel would start the work. Capt. Patterson came over once more. If it was too late for any more battles there might be time for one more skirmish, and Raymond Hood said, "Capt. Patterson, before you sign the contract, there is something I should tell you. I know you have been a good client, and you have let us do nearly everything the way we thought it ought to be done. I don't like to criticize—but on the other hand you are paying me for my advice and I feel I should give it to you."

"Well," said Capt. Patterson, "what's the trouble?"

"In my opinion," continued Hood, "I think you have made two mistakes on this building."

"What are they?"

"One of them is that you made it nine stories on the front instead of three."

"What's the other?" asked the Captain.

"That you want to make the building of brick instead of limestone."

"Well, I'm going to make two more mistakes," declared the Captain.

"What are they?" asked the architect.

"The first one is that we'll keep it nine stories on the front instead of three."

"And what's the second?"

"We'll keep it brick."

As the World Turns

With the lobby to be dark inside, instead of daylighted, the next thing was to decide what to put in it that would be adaptable and of special interest; a newsstand and list of tenants were not enough. So many things were discussed that someone said it looked as if they were trying to put the whole world in there. Whether or not that was the origin of the idea, the final solution was to install an enormous globe, the biggest in New York, to revolve on its polar axis in a deep pit, dramatically illuminated.

The lobby was to be circular, with the globe in the center, and the walls would call for special treatment, with room for cases of varying depths.

Somewhat in the educational spirit of the globe for visitors, the suggestion was made to have various scientific charts and instruments displayed that were concerned with meteorology and the celestial bodies. A map on which the weather patterns would be charted and kept up to the hour would be of daily interest.

At first Capt. Patterson hooted at the idea. "Weather charts!" he snorted. "What the people want are 'murder charts': some kind of a map of the metropolitan area where the latest crimes could be chalked up."

He gave in, however, and Dr. James Henry Scarr of the New York Weather Bureau was invited to take over the project. Pleased to do so, he was given a layout of the cases so he could figure out what to put in them.

Considerable time passed, and then Mr. Hood called me into his office. *The News* had received a call from Dr. Scarr—apparently he was disgusted and ready to throw the whole project over. I was asked to go down and see him. The next afternoon I met Dr. Scarr in his office high in the building overlooking the Battery and the harbor beyond. We became a little better acquainted as he explained the details of a small hurricane that, opportunely, began churning up the waters of the harbor. Then we sat down to his project. I quickly realized the trouble; he had been working a long time on all kinds of schemes and nobody had paid the least attention to what he was doing. In essence, by having certain instruments and scientific models in the cases Dr. Scarr hoped to educate a lot of people about the wind and tide, temperatures, barometric pressures, time and time zones, as well as certain aspects of the earth, the sun and the moon.

One particular piece of apparatus, however, was causing Dr. Scarr some trouble. Within an illuminated globe an oscillating shadow was being contrived to show the portion of the globe in light or darkness at any time during its orbit around the sun. Although he was not an engineer, Dr. Scarr had worked out drawings full of gears and spindles to show how the apparatus would function. The difficulty was in figuring out the train of gears necessary to give the correct number of revolutions of the globe for each oscillation of the shadow.

I wasn't much of an engineer either. "Dr. Scarr," I said, "You know how many times it rotates. Even if you worked it out correctly on the model, nobody looking at it will ever know whether it rotates correctly or not. Wouldn't it be enough just to have a little notice with the explanation on the case stating that the earth rotates so many times per oscillation of the shadow?"

A look of relief came over Dr. Scarr's face. "Young man," he said, "you're worth a thousand dollars to me."

D. PUTNAM BRINLEY

Sketch by Tony Sarg of D. Putnam Brinley, painter of the globe
in the lobby of the *Daily News*
Building.   *courtesy of S.B.A.A.*

In the meantime work was progressing on the great globe. It was made
and erected by Peter Clark, Inc. of New York, especially noted for its work
in stage machinery and equipment. In relation to the floor it was set up on
its polar axis and was provided with proper machinery so that it revolved as
naturalistically as possible. The various geographic and cartographic features were beautifully painted on the surface of the globe by the artist D.
Putnam Brinley.

On the day when the globe was ready for demonstration, Raymond
Hood arranged to meet Capt. Patterson at the lobby, because he wanted the
Captain to be the first to see it. According to Mr. Hood, everything looked
wonderful with the huge illuminated globe, dramatically centered in the
dark lobby, turning around like a celestial orb. Pleased and excited, Raymond Hood nudged Capt. Patterson, "Pretty swell, isn't it?"

Capt. Patterson looked at it a moment or two and then commented,
"It's 'pretty swell' all right, as you say, but it's turning the wrong way."

And so it was. The gears were changed.

Drawing by Hugh Ferris of *Daily News* Building Lobby   *courtesy of Hood family*

Raymond Hood's boyhood
home, Cottage St., Pawtucket.
courtesy of Hood family

Raymond Hood's mother,
Vella Mathewson Hood.
courtesy of Hood family

CHAPTER III

LITTLE ACORNS

Pawtucket to Paris

At the time I came to New York in 1928, Raymond Hood was a well established architect with a busy office on the fourteenth floor of the American Radiator Building at 40 West 40th Street. The partnership had been organized in 1927 under the name of Raymond Hood, Godley and Fouilhoux. Hood had come a long way since he had opened his first little office at 7 West 42nd in 1914, waiting seven long years for the knock on the door.

Raymond Mathewson Hood was born in the mill town of Pawtucket, Rhode Island on March 21, 1881. His mother was Vella Mathewson, who was born on April 8, 1857 and died on September 14, 1919. From her picture, in a beautiful dress, we can see that the family was well-to-do. Another old photograph shows their house on Cottage Street in Pawtucket. It is a commodious shingled house of many gables and balustraded porches in the residential urban style of the nineties.

Hood's great grandfather was the first Baptist Sunday School teacher in Pawtucket. John Parmenter Hood, Raymond's father, was a well-to-do manufacturer of boxes. He brought up his son to be of sterling New

England character and a good Baptist, so good in fact that on his arrival in Paris at the age of twenty-three, young Raymond refused to enter Notre Dame Cathedral because it was a "Catholic" Church. The "hard shell," however, must have been rubbed thin by his sojourn of some six years off and on in Paris as a student of the École des Beaux Arts, for he certainly was a "life of the party" man ever after.

After going through the public schools of Pawtucket, Hood attended Brown University in Providence for two years, 1898 and 1899 before entering the architectural school of the Massachusetts Institute of Technology in Boston. Of those days, Henry H. Saylor, F.A.I.A., editor of the *A.I.A. Journal* and the historian, wrote to E. James Gambaro, F.A.I.A. in 1964:

> "Thanks a million for letting me see the two papers about the Atelier days. Both brought acute spells of nostalgia, for surely there were in these ateliers a spirit and a camaraderie unlike anything that went on before or since. Something that transfigured architectural education. We had something approximating it in the years 1899–1901—and Ray Hood was one of a gang in the architectural department which was as unlike anything in MIT's 13 or 14 courses. The Chemists, Electrical Engineers and all the others undoubtedly thought us crazy, and vice versa. The old Walker Building, just off Copley Square, at night was lighted and heated (so to speak) by the electric bulbs on long extension cords, often rolled up in the folds of a sweater—helping to ward off the absolute zero of a building in which the heat was turned off at night. Bill Crowell, Ellis Lawrence, Redfield Proctor, Roger Greeley, Lovell Little, Andrew Hepburn, to name but a few, were some of the good spirits of that day. Architecture has never been the same, since."

Raymond Hood started work in the office of Cram, Goodhue, and Ferguson, well known Boston architects. According to his partner, Ralph Adams Cram, "not only was Goodhue a very great genius in his own right as a creative artist, he was also a dynamic source of inspiration." Goodhue believed in the coming usage of steel framing and reinforced concrete but not that it was any reason "to throw away stone, and oak, and carving, and metal work, and stained glass." Yet he went on to say, "but I assure you I dream of something very much finer and more modern and more useful to our present day civilization than any Gothic church could possibly be."

When Hood joined the firm, however, it was designing the Church of St. Thomas on Fifth Avenue in New York, and had just won the competition for the United States Military Academy at West Point (1903). For work on the chapel there, Goodhue opened a New York office. Perhaps we attribute too much influence on Raymond Hood at this time to Goodhue, yet this was

Raymond Hood in group photograph (right of shield) as student at Brown University, 1899.   *courtesy of Hood family*

his impressionable period; it was Goodhue who gave Raymond Hood a solid background for his future career. Hood had a short apprenticeship there, for he decided to continue his education at the École des Beaux Arts in Paris, at that time the leading architectural school. As Goodhue himself had had no formal training as an architect it is not surprising that he had little use for academic training for others. Nevertheless, he is said to have advanced his protégé money for the trip, with the admonition *not* to visit Paris *or* go to the École des Beaux Arts. Characteristically, they say, Ray Hood lived up to the letter but dodged the spirit: he didn't go to Paris or the school, he did both.

I do not know to what degree Hood was influenced in his feeling for Gothic architecture by his apprenticeship in Goodhue's office. There is a story that, while he was at M.I.T., the design professor, Mr. Depradelle, had given as a project a church, asking that it be done in the classic style. Because of a certain contrariness in his nature, Raymond Hood did his project in Gothic. Others say that he was just looking ahead; he wanted to have something to show when he applied on graduation for a job in the office of Cram and Goodhue.

Ralph Adams Cram believed the period of thirteenth century English Gothic was the high point of architecture and therein sought his inspiration. His younger partner, Bertram Grosvenor Goodhue, was endowed with the imagination and genius to bring to the style a new vitality and individuality.

Together they were doing some of the best work at the time, and their office was one place a beginner would like to have his start.

Hood's younger friend, Ralph Walker, who followed the same path from Pawtucket to M.I.T. says he doubts if Hood was motivated by any admiration for Gothic as such but by the fact that Goodhue was a magnificent draftsman. In those days there was nothing the student admired more than the man who could draw. At the top of the profession were three superb draftsmen, Goodhue, Henry Hornbostel and Frank Lloyd Wright: the heroes of student worship.

It is interesting that Louis Sullivan, who was also a magnificent draftsman and artist, did not receive the adulation of the M.I.T. students for some reason or other. Yet today, Sullivan is recognized by architectural historians as the father of the first indigenous American theory of architecture, the so-called Chicago School. In recent years students have revered an entirely different type of architect, in particular such men as Le Corbusier, Walter Gropius and Mies van der Rohe, all theorists.

L'École des Beaux Arts

Raymond Hood left for France in 1904, but was unsuccessful in his first try at getting into the Beaux Arts. The subject he failed in was drawing. Some of his life class sketches, one of which is dated August 8, 1904, indicate he attended Calarossi's, one of the best known drawing and painting academies open to art students in this period. It is also known he traveled extensively during this first year abroad, particularly in Italy, spending some time in Rome. This, at least would have pleased Goodhue.

Hood was successful in his second attempt at Beaux Arts and entered the school in the fall of 1905. He was now twenty-four years old. To receive a diploma he would have to complete the requirements before he was thirty years of age. It would be hard from hearsay, and after all these years, to get a clear picture of Hood's life in Paris or his progress in school. One thing handed down is that not only did Ray Hood stay out of "Catholic" cathedrals, at first, that is, but he endeavored to avoid the evils of drink. Finally, however, his French comrades got him started on a bottle of wine and once started, the wine went down with no trouble. But there was just too much of it and his comrades had to carry him home to bed. Hood's Baptist principles were loosening up.

In France, when a boy graduated from high school he was a man of the world and was addressed as "Monsieur." But, thanks to his landlady, this was not the case with Raymond Hood. For an American, he was very small of stature, and the mother instinct must have overcome her. Much to

Classic Detail. Drawing by Raymond Hood, while at Beaux Arts.

courtesy of Hood family

Life class drawings by Raymond Hood at Académie Calarossi, Paris, August, 1904.

courtesy of Hood family

33

Raymond Hood, "Le Jeune Homme" as a student in Paris.
courtesy of Hood family

Raymond's chagrin, she could not bring herself to call him "M'sieur" Hood, but always "Le Jeune Homme," the young man, and so he became known.

This motherly instinct went even further. Although the French were among the first to put in modern plumbing, they were the last people to bring it up to date with modern improvements as long as the original model worked. In a little unheated building in the backyard, the original "convenience" had been installed with a cold, if chaste, marble seat; perhaps "elegant" was the word.

One day young Raymond, in talking to a friend, must have complained about what an ordeal this was to use on a cold winter morning. Apparently the landlady overheard him and somehow or other, from that day on, when "le jeune homme" paid his morning visit the seat was warm. This phenomenon would have remained unexplained but for one of his friends who happened to come by even earlier one morning. Just then the little door opened and out popped the landlady. If her bottom was cold, at least there was a warm seat for "Le Jeune Homme."

34

The above anecdotes were about all that could be gleaned of the Paris years until a packet of letters turned up in the hands of Hood's daughter, Mrs. Trientje Hood Reed. They had been written to a friend, Henry Boehm, from 1905 to 1912. From these we may garner a few more realistic impressions.

As a student, Hood became a member of Atelier Duquesne in 1905. In the Paris system, students were under the tutelage of some well known architect, where they gathered in a studio, or "atelier," generally at night, for criticism by the "patron." Needless to say, there were a number of these ateliers in order to accommodate all the students and there was great competition, with each student hopefully coming under the guidance of the man of his choice. Once admitted to the Atelier Duquesne Ray Hood, innocently, was all but thrown out for good. As a prank, some of the others had locked up, in fact, boarded up, two of their fellow students in a closet. The patron chose this moment to come in.

At first everything was quiet with everyone at work. Then all of a sudden the racket started as the two in the closet realized this was their chance to get out. The patron was infuriated with the disorder and seized on one of the boys as responsible, upbraided him, and threw him out of the atelier. Unfortunately, he had picked a boy who had taken no part in the prank. The "injustice" of it upset Ray Hood so, that in his words, he picked well his moment to tell the patron he had made a mistake. Hood in turn was *enguelé,* "jawed at" by the patron and also put out the door, even if he was an American who couldn't have known any better.

After a few days when things had quieted down, Hood reappeared, to be told he could stay on after all. He did complete the year of study at the Beaux Arts, accumulating a number of points in design. The only letter in this period, dated Vienna, April 23, 1906, indicated he took a vacation of two weeks visiting Costanza and Bucharest. By the 14th of June, Hood was back in New York, where he again went to work for Cram, Goodhue and Ferguson—according to a letter of July 22nd. This letter throws some light on Hood's experience in failing to get into the Beaux Arts the first time. Apparently his friend Henry was experiencing the same treatment and Hood wrote:

> "I am awfully sorry you did not make it—but then I welcome you into the ranks of illustrious men who slipped up in their try—the official title is 'La Société de ceux qui sont tombés dans la merde leur premier essai.' I detest the skulking devils who get in the first crack."

35

Hood wrote that besides working by day in the office:

"All this past week I have been helping Hirons on the Beaux Arts Competition evenings. I think he will surely win it."

Fred Hirons was one of the most accomplished students to come back from the Beaux Arts, and his hand was to be seen in much of the important work done in New York in the years to come.

On September 6, 1906, Hood wrote:

"I have been working since I have been in New York as hard as I ever played in Europe, in earning the three hundred dollars that I find in my pay envelope each week."

Hood was undoubtedly doing well, but certainly not as well as all that.

"New York is boiling over with work of all sorts, principally, however, competitions, so that it is the ideal draughting spot in the world—at least for those in search of lucre."

With the Beaux Arts training based on competition in design projects, any young architect of ability found himself in demand back home with even a year's post graduate work. The letter continues:

"The chief competition is a new Theological Seminary in which about every good firm in New York is competing, fifty in all. Then, after that, comes a school for a million or so in Pittsburgh in which Cram, Goodhue and Ferguson, for whom I am putting in my time, and several others are entered."

Hood's letter continued with his plans concerning Europe:

"I am coming for a couple of months assuredly before July of next year (1907) and possibly even in February. That will be the extent of my trip for this time—but I have decided to finish the École, so that the following year I will have to come back for a longer time. I do not know what right I have to plan thus to do the school, as I haven't a cent of money, but so I am planning quite confidently, and am prepared to bust my G string doing it."

Back and Forth

By October Hood noticed life in New York after a year or two in Paris didn't seem quite the same. Reading his letter of the 28th, it may even be said that it does not seem to have differed from life in the city today:

"First of all I am going to enguèle myself for about three pages for not having written to you in so long a while, which I suppose you have also been doing unless you have completely lost interest in me. But the trouble is all with this 'Sacre nom de Dieu, cochon,' city, where everyone hustles or thinks he hustles so much that he has no time to himself. It is not exactly, however, that you don't have time to yourself—but when you do have it, you are so unnerved and physically debilitated thru having traveled about in subways, then having eaten in pandemonic restaurants, and walked about under thundering elevated trains and thru frenzied crowds—that it is nearly impossible to think of sitting quietly and writing letters. I am afraid my two years abroad has rather unfitted me for hustling New York—if it didn't so get on my nerves before as it does now. There is a tremendous difference between quiet, sedate old Rome, and uproarious New York, and in my present state of mind I much prefer the former. Here, you get out of bed, eat a breakfast—and then submerge yourself in a foul smelling subway—and hanging on to a strap, you are carried three miles downtown to the musical accompaniment of all the dins and crashes which are peculiar to subway travel. Downtown, where you pass the day, is a place in which the sun never penetrates, except by reflection, occasionally, from the thirty-second story windows of the building on the opposite side of the street. Your lunch you eat in a restaurant on the first floor of one of these huge structures, which is necessarily lit by sizzling arc and incandescent lights. The only table vacant is one in the center of the room, so you are in the vortex or maelstrom of feverish, rushing brokers—and then as a touch of local color—or rather local music—thru all the racket and noise you hear the interminable clicking of the ten or twelve stock tickers about the room. Back uptown you go in a delightful way, similar to the way in which you came down—then eat in a place a little less noisy than you were in at noon, but still noisy enough—and then fagged out—to bed. When Sunday comes, you handle yourself like a child—allow yourself to sleep late, eat expensive meals, and try to recuperate yourself for the week following. The whole existence here is a sort of coffee existence—you live on your nerves, which are bolstered and pulled together by black coffee at every meal.

"You may have gathered from this useless hemorrhage, that I do not like New York. Quite right—nom de Dieu, I wish now that that automobile would stop thumping under my window—it has gone off now, so that I can hear more distinctly the steel workers on the apartment house across the street."

From that letter we learn that some three weeks before, Hood had left Goodhue's office; in his employer's eyes, Ray Hood must have become "tainted" by his academic education after all. He was fired, they tell us, and was "all broken up" about it. Hood left for Pittsburgh to work for Henry Hornbostel as his chief designer. Continuing in Hood's letters, we read.

"As for news, the principal event in my existence is that since three weeks I have been with your old master, Hornbostel, where I have a job that pleases me very much, if I can only hold on to it. I have had nothing but competition work to do, and there is still a lot more of it ahead, so naturally, I am very much contented—as competitions are very much less 'enmerdant' than working drawings. As for going back to Paris, I have definitely killed all chance of that until next June at least, by moving into an apartment house which has bay trees in the front lobby—and elevator boys with buttons. While the ten million or so dollars a month rent, which we pay, is a mere bagatelle, still it is sufficient to make me sure that I will not be back in Paris, for eight months, at least."

With the start of the year 1907 Ray Hood is still in Pittsburgh working for Hornbostel on the finals of the Albany competition, a $7,000,000 project. It is believed that this competition, won by Hornbostel, was for the State Education Department, including a library referred to later. Other work was for the new buildings for the Carnegie Technical Schools, again a competition won by Hornbostel:

"It is a lovely soft job and makes me think of the way we used to work in Rome—except when Hornbostel is here himself, and then I always get a solid belly full of work. . . . He can give Emperor Wilhelm or Roosevelt points on how to do two weeks work every day."

Hood goes on to write:

"I am awfully sorry about the tangle you and Ruch (?) had with the last exams. Did you do what Hirons and I did, one time, sit together and give one another criticisms? We told one and another all through the day what good things we had, and then had the pleasure of receiving two 'bons riens.' The next exam we made a point of keeping apart."

38

New York may have seemed a stifling place to live after Paris, but the sojourn in Pittsburgh eased up on that impression. In February Hood wrote from that city;

"I am still submerged in the cloud of smoke trying to be content. I go back to New York this week, though—and I will actually like the city after my experience here."

Hood always seemed to be short of cash. From the letters we begin to get an idea of how he felt about money and perhaps why he never could hold on to it. He continues:

"A great event—I have been able to save forty dollars. All I have to save is three hundred dollars more before June first—and as I saved the forty dollars in six months the rest will be easy."

There were three months to go.

"How is that for pure, undefiled faith,—for I really think I am going to Paris in June. That is the sort of faith that moves mountains—the kind I was taught about when I was young."

Hood must have made it for a short trip as indicated by a letter dated July 15, 1907:

"My last week in Paris was quite up to the former standard I had set —if you have any evil anticipations about them—they were fully real-ized—in a strictly virtuous way, however."

On his return, Hood is no sooner off the boat when, that same night, a frightfully hot August night, he takes the sleeper to Albany to meet Horn-bostel. He doesn't complain because he is given a job to do he likes—to start the work, alone, on the library at Albany. This project is not only a large one, but as such, interesting as well.

He speaks of meeting one Harry Adler and discussing love in its various forms. Continuing in translation:

"He has been able to give me information on my lady friend. Of what he had they only speak well of her except that she knows how to spend money like a millionaire. She lets it run like water. Beside her it seems there are very few women in New York who are better instructed in the art of spending—mon dieu—I knew if before—even so—I will have to be careful. I have not seen her yet because she has been in Newport since my return."

Further along he says:

"As for my studies in Paris, I don't know what to do. I have a tremendous desire to return—but I fear it may be quite simply for the pleasures of life over there and to avoid the work here—rather than a true desire to study more. If that is the case, I would be wrong to touch my father for a sum sufficient for two or three years. He has already given me a good education, and now I cannot ask that he support me when I am only a dilettante who amuses himself in Paris. At this moment I believe I will not come back—but naturally only to the point that I do not lose my place in the school, I will never be sure. I will always have the wish but it will be necessary that I first convince myself that I am honest. . . ."

In another letter Hood writes an interesting commentary on his own character:

"You will forgive me for not writing a more personal letter—but my temperament seems absolutely to forbid my writing you as personal a one as I should like to. I have never been able to write, even to my mother, a letter with the slightest sympathy in it, or with a character distinct from one I would write to any other person."

The next letter gives some further sidelights on Ray Hood's concern, or rather lack of concern about money matters. He writes:

"Of the fifty dollars that I owed Burnham—I had forty all together—and was waiting merely for the last ten—when I wrote, when—poof! about thirty of it went the way you may have seen me let it go in Paris —once or twice. Then came a letter from Burnham saying 'send it any old time you like'—on which I put a *very* loose construction. Then came your letter saying you would pay my debt and that I might pay it to your brother—and my good resolutions vanished. I told your brother that I owed *him* fifty dollars and promptly put it out of my mind. From beginning to end a most dastardly piece of trust-busting finance!"

"But my conscience has been bothering me lately—and now I am about to pay your brother. That is to say—I have the check all made out to him and all I have to do is to deposit the fifty dollars to meet it. Which thing, so help me, I am going to do this Saturday."

From this same letter of October 27, 1907 we learn more of Hood's indecision about returning to Paris to finish school.

"As regards what you said about my not coming back to Paris—altho I am still as undecided as before, in case I should not come back, it would not be a result of a lack of nerve, or from a financial point of view—altho quite properly that enters into it to a certain extent. The conditions rather are these—I am placed exceptionally well in New York—being placed in charge of a big building and working under a very strong man, who is disposed to teach me all he can, and who is now in the height of his enthusiasm. From a professional point—I very much doubt if I would learn as much in Paris, as I will here, as the work I would do there would not be as big, nor permit of any greater play of imagination than the work I have here. The chief value of two years in Paris, would be in having two quiet years in which to *think* and to order my present rather hurly-burly life. Now, a great deal of my energy is very probably misdirected thru a lack of a definite plan and forethought. My method for progress is no more precise than this—to do everything that comes up as thoroughly and as hard as possible—and not to miss an opportunity—to work blindly but hard—in a few words. And in New York one falls too easily into the habit of working without thinking on account of the amount of work that there is to do. Paris should be a corrective for that.

"One real danger in staying here is of falling too much under the influence of one man—of imitating rather than learning—for no matter how strong a man may be one must unquestionably avoid being swallowed up.

"Financially—it would mean my going in debt for my time in Paris— but that I should not hesitate to do, could I be firmly convinced that Paris is the better place for me.

"Leaving aside the consideration that I like Paris and would like to live there—that states the case fairly I think. Now I have much to choose between two paths—with at present not the slightest idea as to which I should follow."

From the letter written in March, 1908, we learn that Hood is still working on competitions, in fact, just starting on one of them for Sing Sing prison. But there is still the question in his mind when he writes to Henry asking the date of the "en loge," the start of the May project. Is it one to be met if he is to keep his place in school? The age limit is thirty; he asks if they mean until you're thirty or just before you reach thirty-one. He writes:

"It is only a question of math as I have all my values in architecture— but I will be twenty-seven at the end of this month and I do not think the routine of the school will allow me to finish before I am thirty. Further I am still undecided about coming back next year."

Finally, Hood decides to return and a letter of July 30, 1908 comes from Paris, "I still have several things to do including a 'loge' tomorrow."

By the 22nd of August Hood has finished his trigonometry and is "part way through the analytique." By September he is taking math twice a day with the additional note, "I got a check from a man in Providence for 250 francs and spent it."

A little later he writes he is studying math from 9 a.m. to 7 at night: "that's an achievement, I am doing my Pelee plates of which I do one or two a day." By the end of the year he gave up a trip to Switzerland because the math exams were imminent. However, "I am going to try and not be a fool with my time and money, so that I can go off to Spain in the spring."

The year 1909 seems to have been one of extensive traveling, England, Switzerland, and Italy. Both his brother Arthur and his father visited and travelled with him. Hood writes of over-eating at friend Webster's in Paris in December, but the next letter is dated June 1, 1910 from Pawtucket. It includes the note, "The family understands I have a *girl* in Paris. What do you think of that?"

In a letter of August 21, 1910 we find out that Hood is working on a Maritime Bourse, in Normandie Gothic, getting his inspiration from the Palace of Justice in Rouen. The time has come, however, for him to submit a subject for his final project for his diploma. For this "diplôme" he has decided on a City Hall for his home town in Pawtucket R.I.:

"The town for which I made a sketch a long while ago, you remember. I have worked a little on it and the subject has quite "emballé" the patron. I suppose he likes it because it is not a maison de Campagne."

The copy of this drawing was obtained from the year book of the Rhode Island Chapter of the A.I.A. for the year 1911.

Finishing Up

In his letter of October 24, 1910 to Henry Boehm, again in French, Hood writes:

"You will excuse me if I commence with the important news—from my point of view—it is that I have finished the school. For the bourse, the project, I worked like a dog. I came out with a first medal, and with that a prize, le prix Cavel, which they gave for the first time for the one who makes first place for the summer project but the prize, which is 300 francs, became very complicated when it became a matter of awarding it. In the first place, there was a fellow from a regional school, the Garnier Atelier in Lyons, who turned in an enormous project—including everything—with steam boats, sail boats in the foreground, tug boats, lighthouses, dock yards, the Bourse (Stock Exchange) perched on a wall 30 meters high with immense stairs and ramps, which gave access to a little custom house below—a real collection of all the past maritime competitions of the school—with impressive borders and titles. Naturally he is classed "premier empetant avec plusiers doigts dans le cul"—it was a first medal of the first class. But the unhappy wretch, with all that, was not able to have the prize because he is not of the school, properly speaking, but of a regional school.

Project for "Diplôme" at the École des Beaux Arts—City Hall for Pawtucket by Raymond Hood.
from yearbook, 1911, Rhode Island Chapter of A.I.A.

"Consequently, being the only other one to have a first medal, and being from the school, I picked up the award—but with the title of 'foreigner'—when the count was over it was Delaou of Laloux's who collected the three hundred francs with a first second medal.

"Anyway that made up my ten points, and I have nothing to complain
of. I have already written you, I believe, that I did it in Gothic, but that
was not pleasing to the Harvards who are at Duquesne's at this time because it was not pure in style—that sinks me—but I will send you a copy
of it as soon as Vincent gives it to me. . . .

"Here nothing much happens. The Atelier goes well—the Americans
in the Atelier behave so well that they have grouped themselves apart—
in the small room, we hear nothing from them except the sound of pencils from morning to night and the result at the end of the week is some
fifteen or so great plans which are exciting to look at—for a minute, but
unnecessary to ever look at them much more. The more I see them work,
the more I ask myself why they do not wish to travel and see a little of
what goes on around them. They are coming to pass a year in Europe—
for the only time, and immediately they shut themselves up in an atelier
for six months—they are afraid I think, there is not enough to see to
keep them busy. However, that is their business.

"I have now begun my diplôme—a city hall for Pawtucket—I will
have been able to make a little 'm—e' for the November submission—but
I prefer to do it a little more properly for February, and even more I
could still work in school competitions."

There must have been a fire or burglary for which insurance was paid:

"From 38 rue de Sevres—I have had a rather funny incident. I found
out they have indemnified all the boarders in the house—except Mrs. Sellier, and myself—it was when we went to the Bon Marché to make a
claim the director told us—'Mrs. Sellier you have no need for the money
and as for Mr. Hood—he is a foreigner—if that doesn't please you—it's
too bad.' In other words, the Bon Marché told us 'nous en envoyer
ch—r.' Naturally we were furious, but without making a long case of it
a lawyer told us there is nothing we could do. The filthy wretches! . . ."

Hood goes on to note:

"Duquesne leaves in March for America where he is to stay two or
three months to organize *Harvard*. At least that is what he says, although
everyone seems to think he is going for good."

Quoting from an early account of the school, furnished by Miss Shill-
aber, librarian of the School of Architecture at Harvard:

44

"In 1911 also an important addition was made by the calling of Professor Eugene Joseph Armand Duquesne, a graduate of the Beaux Arts and winner of the Grand Prix de Rome, to teach Design.

"The Great War interfered with the development of the Schools. Professor Duquesne had a great success, but was recalled to France in 1914 and was not able to return."

According to a story, no professor's salary at Harvard would have been adequate to induce the great man to come, so President A. Lawrence Lowell voluntarily added half of his own to the largest one available to make it worth his while. The coming of the distinguished Frenchman was widely heralded and the ladies of Cambridge looked forward, not without some rivalry amongst themselves, to his coming. He came, he fulfilled his mission, but he remained a true Frenchman at heart. He made the most of his American venture financially, but hardly graced a social occasion, saving every cent that he could of his magnificent salary to put into his canvas sock and carry back to France. Of course, all this may be malicious gossip.

Describing more of the life of the atelier at this time,

"Carlu did the prix American again, another stupid subject, airport for dirigibles, aeroplanes, submarines, etc. for coast defense. He got a mention, and tied with LeMoninée /?/ of Herands /?/ for second place. The whole concours though was a howling failure, as was to be expected from a purely military (project) treated by an architect. The winner had a facade five metres long—a cliff, with a battery of guns in one corner, and a warship in front. It appears he got the prize because it gave the impression of being impregnable. Next they will probably give a coal mine as a subject.

"I am just starting my 'diplôme' on white paper. It is the limit for size, facade and coupe each eight feet high, one plan double grand aigle, six grand aigle sheets. I am having Magnette burn candles to the Virgin in order that I get through. It finishes February 18, and two weeks after that, I will start for home—not that I want to—but it will be time."

From another package of letters written from abroad by Raymond's older brother J. Lawrence Hood, we learn that this plan of return was not carried out. Lawrence Hood, who was married and had two or three small children, lived in South Attleboro, Massachusetts. About this time he made a trip abroad, travelling with Raymond.

The following account is from *Travel* January 1912 by Lawrence Hood. In an adventurous spirit the two brothers took the horse drawn "Poste" over the Simplon Pass in winter, instead of going through it by train:

The last train for the night had gone, so the station master very kindly put out the lights, and together we three picked our way along the narrow road to a little hotel about a mile up into the quiet stillness of the Alps. A satisfying repast, real Swiss honey and Italian wine, and we tumbled into a cold, cold bed, thankful that the bedclothes were at least a foot thick. We couldn't have existed with less.

The morning sun was magnificent, but we made what seemed a proper deduction and figured that if it was cold at Iselle, what would the answer be at the Hospice, 6,500 feet above the sea. For sundry reasons, therefore, we dressed with our nightshirts tucked deep in our trousers, put on four suits of underclothes, six pairs of stockings, five vests, twenty-three stick-pins and eighty-seven collar buttons, and decided that we were prepared. . . .

The "Poste" did not leave until ten A.M., so we had ample time to go and see the entrance of the Simplon Tunnel on the Italian side. . . .

Plenty of blankets, a sort of scoot wind shield, a long round lead tank filled with boiling hot water and wrapped up in straw in the bottom of the "Poste" kept us comfortable. We soon came to the Swiss Custom House, where the "papers" and our baggage were examined with all the dignity and decorum of a real port of entry. "Have you any cigars, vin, or tabac?" is the prevailing question at any continental frontier. . . .

A power plant at Iselle and also one at Brigue at the Swiss entrance of the tunnel, alternately driving or pulling air through one tunnel and using the other as a circulating medium, keep the air sailing through the shaft in a gale. After the air has completed its long journey it is rather hot and comes rushing out into the open like the smoke from a steam engine.

On the Italian side of the boundary between the two countries there is a wide wooden bridge in the pass, which if removed would render passage by an invader almost impossible, especially in view of the fact that the mountain side bristles with port-holes from which a rain of shot and shell could rake the pass from top to bottom.

You must imagine more or less the scenery—it would almost be a pity for me to impose on its grandeur with an apology for a description. We wind in and out between the cracks of the mountains, first clear down to the bottom, then way up on a cliff with a yawning abyss below, and only a few rocks set in the side of the road to prevent us from crashing down to destruction. But the horses seem to have a very careful regard for their own safety, so we therefore do not spend much time worrying. Above us the mountains are covered with snow, and below, the Alpine stream rushes and tumbles over the ragged rocks. . . .

Soon the road bed is snow instead of gravel and we come suddenly upon a two-seated sled to which we transfer bag and baggage and to

(*Left*) Raymond and the "Poste" preparing to cross the Simplon Pass with his brother Lawrence, winter, 1911. *Right:* Crossing the Pass, with Raymond out front.

courtesy of Hood family

which we hitch our horses single file instead of abreast. The change gives us a chance to look back, and we see the precipitous mountains between which we have passed. They remind one of our American El Capitan, rising so sheer as to be absolutely bare of snow. . . .

The descent to Brigue now began. We had had three horses in single file drawing us. Now one was enough, and the other two followed loose behind. The snow was fifteen feet deep and the pass ran right along on a little shelf of snow on the precipitous side of the mountain. We could look down two to three thousand feet at a breathless angle which would take your breath away, and to the edge of this descent one need take but a single step from the side of the sled. . . .

At one point on the shelf of snow a small snow-slide had come down the mountain side and filled our narrow path. One of the drivers went ahead and dug it out with his feet lest we should be tipped over and landed deep out of sight in some unknown chasm of snow far below. It was perfectly still and the snow seemed packed down very solid, but as we waited for the path to be cleaned, we wondered what would be the

47

sensations if such a snow-slide should come rushing down and catch our little outfit en route. But we were soon traveling again, lost to everything except that magnificent picture of white.

The Simplon Pass was made really serviceable by order of Napoleon Bonaparte. In the winter, with the snow fifteen feet deep, the pass is of course up above the regular roadbed, and it is, perhaps, a little dangerous on account of a possible snow-slide. Perhaps if the snow were not solid it might give way under you, but to provide for such danger the government always has a few men working along the route all the time to keep it passable and as safe as possible. . . .

The letters Lawrence wrote home to his wife Martha also described the tour in careful attention to detail and with enthusiasm for what they saw, especially the scenery. While the letters generally relate to what "we" the two brothers did, occasionally there are specific references to Ray.

The first letter, dated March 6th, 1911 describes the trip by train from Marseilles to Rome, with exciting views of the Riviera. Lawrence and Ray stopped over in Nice and made a side trip to Monte Carlo . . . :

"By showing his passport, Ray got tickets of admission for both of us and we were in the den of gamblers. You should see them drop as high as $200.00 at a clip without a whimper. The money flowed like water. I will describe the method when I get home. At least as many women gambled as men and some of them just as recklessly."

They were a long way from South Attleboro, Mass. Lawrence and Ray continued their trip through Genoa and Pisa to Rome. Noting that the Coliseum served as a stone quarry for many of the churches, including St. Peter's, Lawrence raised this question:

"First, is it not too bad that the marvelous old structures of the Romans could not have been left?—or second, is the magnificence we now see with its stolen pillars, carvings, pictures, etc., etc., even more wonderful than the old would have been had it been left untouched?"

He goes on to say,

"The excavations are much larger than when Ray was here before and on Palatine Hill you can roam through the rooms and halls of the old Roman Emperors."

Commenting on the current theater Lawrence noted,

"The theaters of Rome are poor. I went to one where half the floor space was devoted to chairs, tables, etc. for restaurant purposes and where

48

the backs of the rest in front of you had a shelf so you could be served anytime, and where you could wear your hat while the show went on if you wanted to, where they talked a little to an actor if they wanted to and talked among themselves most any old time—a real free and easy occasion—if there happened to be more interest in the conversation or if they happened to be especially enjoying their wine, they didn't bother to clap.

"The way the hack men swing their whips would scare you for fear anybody within reach might get hit, and actually Ray and I had to ask one driver to confine his whip to his horse and leave us alone. . . .

"We arrive in Paris Sat. night the 18th at 11 p.m. The plan is this. Ray wants to get his diplôme into the Salon. He will need until the 25th to get it ready. So my plan is to leave him in Paris alone so he can have full benefit of the week 18th to 25th. I'm going over to London alone and spend the week thereabout. We have changed our plan of ship because it fits all the conditions much better. It is this. We shall sail from Havre on the 25th on the La Lorraine. She docks in New York City on Sat. April 1st not sooner than 10 a.m. So plan to come down and meet us. . . ."

Upon his final return to America in 1911, Hood returned to Pittsburgh to work for Henry Hornbostel as his chief designer. In May he was out on a construction job, presumably Carnegie Tech. The contractor was on a salary as was the architect Hornbostel. Ray Hood was then working on specifications, earning a good salary and gaining business and practical experience.

In August, Hood was back in town. Writing again to Henry Boehm he relates,

"I have no news in particular save that the past two Sundays I have poisoned myself with fresh country air."

In September:

"Still eating my young life away at the Schenley Hotel. As for my work, we are going to begin building in a month so things are getting busy."

November:

"After having one building nearly finished Hornbostel returned from the west with his mind full of changes and what started out to be a very carefully studied building, has developed into his usual charette at the end—tant pis"

In his letter of May 7th, 1912 from Pittsburgh, Raymond Hood notes that Prof. Duquesne came out for the cornerstone laying of the Carnegie Technical School—apparently "quite an event." This was the last of the Henry Boehm letters.

Today from Henry Hornbostel's son, Caleb, a small boy at the time, we glean a little information about his father's office. Their practice depended on winning competitions and Henry Hornbostel gathered a fine group of artists about him. Charles Keck, the sculptor, was one of them and he stayed with the firm until he died. He was responsible for the sculpture on the State Education Building in Albany. Keck became one of Hood's life long friends. Successful in his investment, the wealthier Keck was able to help out his impecunious friend from time to time. The firm's name was Palmer and Hornbostel; it later became Palmer, Hornbostel and Plonsky. Hood and Plonsky were great friends even to the extent of running after the same model, "Violette."

As there were then few architectural schools in the country at that time, architects' offices provided the training for beginners and they tended, on the average, to stay with an office as apprentices rather longer than they do today.

Although the work of this office is associated with the "classic" or "Beaux Arts" style it was nevertheless progressive in its outlook, making many forward looking contributions to architectural practice. One example is the State Education Building in Albany. In the Beaux Arts tradition such a building called for a monumental staircase to face the visitor on entering. The fact that it only went to the second floor, regardless of the number of stories, was of little consequence. Hood and Hornbostel realized the elevator was actually the important means of circulation in the modern American building, so their entrance leads to the elevator lobby directly, the main stair being at one side.

As early as 1910 Mr. Hornbostel was using mercury-vapor lights in the Soldiers and Sailors Memorial from experience with them in a school. He used the conventional coffered ceiling as a light source, filling the coffers with glass and using lights above. Even the classic cornice was to have tube lighting above it—the beginning of cove lighting. It was in this tradition-breaking atmosphere that Hood gained his practical experience. At the end of three years he decided the time had come for him to start out on his own. According to Caleb Hornbostel, Hood was determined to become "the greatest architect in New York." Having expressed this ambition, he left Pittsburgh for the big city.

CHAPTER **IV**

THE NEW YORK ARCHITECT

The Shingle Hangs Out

In 1914 Raymond Hood returned to New York and, together with another young architect, Rayne Adams, set up an office on the top floor of an old brownstone at 7 West 42nd St. There was little to do except listen for footsteps on the stairs. They were few and far between. To keep busy, Hood started to cover the walls of the front office with gilt paper, but the money ran out before it was done. Enough was finished, however, to earn it the name of "Hood's Gold Room." The significance of this room may be that it revealed a leaning towards the use of gold—which again appeared on the American Radiator Building on Bryant Park a few years later.

It was not that Hood didn't have important clients, when they came. It was just that they seemed to come to him with small jobs. For Mrs. White-law Reid he was asked to fix up a bathroom in the Westchester Farms estate, in anticipation of a visit by the Prince of Wales. Hood's solution for the problem of a crack in the wall was—"Hang a picture over it." This saved her all of $12 to have the crack patched.

Mrs. Reid must have been pleased with his work, however, for she continued to give Hood odd jobs, including superintending the removal of eight bodies from an old tomb on the grounds to a new one outside.

All of this hardly sufficed to "keep body and soul together." According to Caleb Hornbostel, Hood pieced out a living by working on competitions for other architects, among them Henry Hornbostel. If Hood had to content himself with such small jobs as came his way his sights, at least, were ever high. From the *Providence Sunday Journal* of March 16, 1916 we have a glimpse of what Raymond Hood would do if he had a chance. In bold headlines in the "Special Features" section we read:

A STRIKING PLAN FOR DIGNIFYING CIVIC CENTRE

"Former Rhode Islander suggests Imposing State and Municipal Group with Tower, to Occupy Entire Square South of Exchange Place."

This article goes on to say:

"Startling, ambitious and comprehensive are the plans that have been drawn by Raymond M. Hood, a New York architect, as a suggestion for an improvement of Exchange Place, with the ultimate object of making the great plaza one of the most beautiful squares in America.

"For a number of years those interested in making Providence a city beautiful have devoted considerable study to possible methods of taking full advantage of the possibilities of beautifying the great civic centre, but perhaps none of the plans thus far devised has been quite as ambitions, quite as comprehensive or quite as flexible as those suggested by Mr. Hood."

Continuing further on:

". . . the new courthouse, in the form of a great round tower, would be placed in the middle of the area midway between Exchange Street and Dorrance Street, facing Exchange Place. This tower would be flanked on both sides by lower buildings, that near Dorrance Street being connected with City Hall by a tunnel and, possibly, that at the east end of the block with the Federal building in the same way.

"He regards Exchange Place as the logical and ideal location. It is easily accessible to offices of lawyers in the heart of the down-town district. Others having business in the court coming into the city on steam trains and trolley cars would be conveyed almost to the main entrance by these mediums of transportation. The cost of the land for the site of the courthouse itself would not be much greater than the expense entailed for the same purpose in other sections."

The scheme includes several forward looking and imaginative ideas.

Newspaper article
courtesy of Hood family

Drawing by Raymond Hood, August, 1915, for a Court House in proposed Civic Center for Providence, R.I.

courtesy of Pencil Points

Quoting Raymond Hood the article says:

"The present tracks of the steam railroad would cross this boulevard underground, eliminating the present heavy grade in the road bed. Land now occupied by the freight yards, together with the area already owned by the city, would provide sites for public buildings in the future, including the auditorium, should it be deemed inadvisable to locate it on Exchange Place."

The article goes on to say that, in drawing his plans Mr. Hood had placed the courthouse well back from the street and the courtrooms would be some distance above the travelled way, thereby eliminating the annoyance of traffic noises. This theory had been proved by large commercial buildings, in which the occupants on the upper floors were never annoyed despite the fact that such buildings were located upon streets with much noisier pavements than that in Exchange Place.

Again quoting Raymond Hood the article says:

"Architecturally and sentimentally the approach to Providence from the bay and the surrounding country, with the white dome of the State House and the huge marble shaft of the courthouse dominating the city would be admirable. The round form was adopted for this as well as for practical reasons.

"A square tower in America has lost its monumental significance through its use in so many commercial buildings, whereas a round tower, fundamentally uncommercial in form, and one requiring the space and location that can be given only to public buildings is the one form of a tower that will always retain its individual character.

"From the mass of rectangular buildings, this building would always detach itself and hold its place as does the tower of Galatea over the city of Constantinople. From the point of view of construction the round tower is a more rigid type than the rectangular tower, and a study of the typical floor plan will show how admirably it adapts itself to the needs of a courthouse.

"The tower itself is 100 feet in diameter and approximately 600 feet high. The State offices and the office for the Attorney General, etc. occur in the low part of the building over the loggia. At the terrace level the tower is open, forming a huge open air vestibule with the general vestibule of the building over it.

"Above this are one office floor and nine courtroom floors each 26 feet high with two courtrooms, judges and witness rooms on each floor. Above these nine stories behind the small columnade occurs a law library occupying the entire floor. The circular form of this room gives a reading space against the lighted outside wall of 250 feet in length with a

54

five-story radial stack in the centre. Above the law library is a detention prison in which the radial cell system in five tiers would be used.

Like many another noble scheme this one, too, was doomed to be lost in the shuffle of time and never heard of again.

Mori's Restaurant and Hood's Marriage

Hood had some other work from time to time, alterations for the most part. This was never enough to shift him out of low gear, or even keep him from stalling. However, towards the end of this period Hood had a lucky break: a restaurant keeper named Placido Mori had enough confidence in him to let him have his meals on the cuff when his pocket proved empty. Even though Hood was now forty, Mori had picked him for a winner. As he said at the time, "He must be a genius—he eats so much." Mori even gave Hood a job—some say to get his money back, or at least in lieu of rent for the small apartment he let him use—remodeling his establishment, the famous Mori's Restaurant on Bleecker Street, Greenwich Village. It is said no restaurant served better wines and liquors in those difficult days of prohibition, available only to a "trusted" part of the clientele. The unlikely entrance to the "restricted" area was through a telephone booth in the men's room of the establishment next door.

The apartment which Mori made available to his impecunious boarder apparently provided not only shelter but even lent Hood an air of substance. He soon became engaged and, on October 25th, 1920, Hood married his beautiful secretary, Elsie Schmidt. On the strength of a small job designing radiator covers for the American Radiator Company, they moved to an apartment in one of the old houses on Washington Square. The ceilings were so high that two levels were possible in the height of the living room, permitting an upper level bedroom with a kitchen below.

The only reason they left, according to Papa Hood, was that "the bureau drawers wouldn't hold any more babies." Soon all this was to change.

Back in 1847 the first four hundred copies of a newspaper called the *Chicago Tribune* were printed on a hand press for distribution in a small town of 16,000 people. Seventy-five years later, printing 4,000,000 *Tribunes* a week, the newspaper company was ready to build for that city of commensurate growth, "the ultimate in civic expression—the world's most beautiful office building." On June 10th, 1922, the *Chicago Tribune* announced the world-wide *Tribune* Tower Competition for the design of the structure. Ten American architects were invited to compete. One of them, John Mead Howells, asked Raymond Hood to go into the competition with him.

Two hundred sixty-three designs were received from all over the world. On December 23, 1922 the decision of the jury was announced:

Design Number 69

by JOHN MEAD HOWELLS
and RAYMOND M. HOOD
New York

First Prize . . . $50,000

Penniless and heavily in debt Raymond Hood borrowed some more money to buy a decent coat and went out to Chicago to receive the award. I imagine Placido Mori was happy, too. On Hood's return, the first thing his wife Elsie did was to borrow his check, hire a taxi and then drive around to all their creditors to let them know that their ship had, at last, come in.

The Chicago Tribune Competition

Winning the competition was no small achievement. According to the architectural historian Dr. Walter L. Creese, it was the most important single event of the 1920–1930 era, as well as being the first important architectural competition since the war. The American skyscraper captured the imagination of all and the search for the best expression of the new type of building proved to be of great international interest as well.

Over two hundred and fifty entries were received before the competition closed on December 1st, 1922: including fifty-four from twenty-three foreign countries. Through the efforts of the *Chicago Tribune,* the results were given the widest publicity throughout the world and a travelling exhibition of 135 drawings, also prepared by the *Tribune,* was displayed in 27 cities. From almost complete obscurity and literally overnight the name of Raymond Hood achieved the prominence that comes to only a few architects.

The award was not without suspense. A period of one month's grace after the nominal closing date had been allowed to give foreign entries time to arrive. From the works already on hand the jury and the advisory committee had tentatively selected twelve designs. With December 1st the absolute closing date, a design from Finland, numbered 187, cleared customs on November 29th to come in under the wire. It was so striking it jumped ahead of all the other entries, except number 69, to second place. Number 187 had been submitted by Eliel Saarinen of Helsingfors.

When the drawings were published, many architects, as well as the architectural press, thought this second prize by Saarinen should have won. It was indeed a beautiful design, and Raymond Hood was the first to regret that it was not the winner, so impressed was he by its obvious merits. However, the simple rules of the competition had asked for only two things, the first that it be a beautiful and distinctive building, and secondly, that it be highly functional to serve the purposes of the various departments and offices of the newspaper, exclusive of the printing plant. A careful analysis of plans and sections reveals the superiority of the winning scheme in this regard. As for the exterior, both designs expressed the idea of the skyscraper in a vertical treatment: the one by Howells & Hood in the familiar Gothic, Saarinen's in more of an original and imaginative detail. Both were "monumental"—massive in character.

The Saarinen design had some influence on contemporary American design for a time. One of the transcriptions, the San Francisco Telephone Headquarters Building by Timothy Pflueger, carried out the details almost literally. If anything, this served to show that as beautiful as they appeared

The *Chicago Tribune* Building. Rendering by Birch Burdette Long.

Chicago Tribune Building Competition. Submissions by Max Taut (*left*) and Gropius & Meyer (*right*)   *courtesy of* Chicago Tribune

in the rather "atmospheric" rendering, the details lacked the vitality in stone that they indicated in pencil.

The *Tribune* published a volume illustrating some 160 of the designs received. A glance through the pages illustrates the universal interest in the new form of architecture—the American skyscraper. There is little doubt, however, that few had found a successful solution to its design as a composition: the presentations of Howells & Hood, Eliel Saarinen, and Holabird & Roche looked surprisingly well in comparison. Almost all were trying for the "beautiful" building called for by the owner and were influenced by the broad hints in the press that this meant "classic." A few Europeans, however, considering the skyscraper a building calling for an American architecture, recognized the indigenous approach in the work of Louis Sullivan and other American architects, and expressed the same feeling. One such design was that of Max Taut, another by Walter Gropius and Adolph Meyer, both submissions from Germany.

To architectural historians no American design showed any recognition of the work of the group that included Louis Sullivan, which came to be known as the "Chicago School." Yet in later years as this approach developed in Europe it was to come back to America as modern architecture in the age of steel and glass office buildings.

Many of the original pencil sketches by Raymond Hood indicating the steps in the development of the design have been saved. They show an early conception of his idea for the building and then a continuous and unwavering development to the completed design, which was very finished in detail compared to many of the other submissions. As Ely Jacques Kahn said later:

"Looking over the drawings of the *Chicago Tribune* Building competition, it is easy to see why Hood's scheme won out. There was clarity and logic in plan and mass. The fact that his detail was Gothic amused him some years later, for, as he put it quite tersely himself, the building was erected when embroidery was in vogue, and he was more concerned with the actual structure than its shell."

While the broad hints of the owner may have implied a "classic" style was desired, "Gothic" was also traditional and acceptable, well established in religious buildings and fine residences. The Woolworth Building in 1914 by Cass Gilbert had proved it an even more adaptable style for sky-scrapers. There was no question of its acceptability in the competition.

Judging by his work in the competition, we find Raymond Hood a competent architect, a skilled planner with a good sense of beauty and proportion, and a dyed-in-the-wool conservative anxious to interpret the equally conservative point of view of his new client.

His success in winning the competition, however, did not insure Hood the job of making the plans for the construction of the building. Although Col. McCormick was perfectly willing to broadcast the name of Howells & Hood as the winners, it was, to him, only as winner of the $50,000 prize. The program did not say the winner would also be the architect of the building. It said, "if selected by the Owner as architect for the building"—he would enter into contract. In this case, apparently, Col. McCormick had no intention of letting an inexperienced architect, unheard of up to the moment, assume responsibility for the final plans. Then began what Raymond Hood later said was the greatest battle of his life—to convince a tough and stubborn character, Robert R. McCormick, that he could and should do the job. He succeeded.

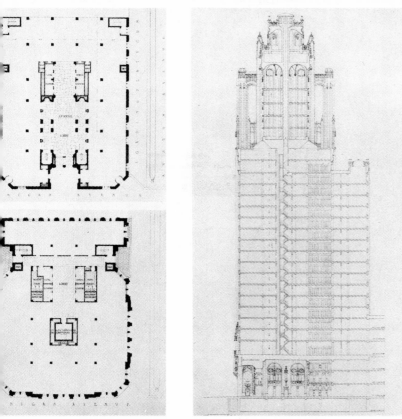

First Prize, Howells & Hood

CHICAGO TRIBUNE BUILDING COMPETITION

Second Prize, Eliel Saarinen   *courtesy of* Chicago Tribune

Detail sketch by Raymond Hood for top of *Chicago Tribune* Building. *courtesy of Hood family*

(opposite page) Photograph of the *Chicago Tribune* Building *courtesy of Bill Engdahl, Hedrich-Blessing*

Chicago Tribune Building as completed by Howells and Hood. Rendering by Hugh Ferris.

Within the Concept of His Time

The great post-war building period of the skyscraper from 1922 to 1930 was ushered in by the *Chicago Tribune* Competition. The career of Raymond Hood was to coincide almost exactly with this period. It may be of interest, therefore to consider certain developments in American architecture, pertaining particularly to work in the Eastern part of the country. The first of these was the education of the architect.

By the 1890's America was a rapidly growing country with a vast amount of building to do. But there were few architectural schools to which an ambitious student, anxious to get a sound professional education, could go. The majority received their training as apprentices in the offices of established architects. The best known architectural school was the École des Beaux Arts in Paris, which Raymond Hood attended. The Beaux Arts welcomed students from all countries for education at the public expense, although there was some limit on the number of foreigners accepted. American students attended in ever increasing numbers up to 1914 and the First World War.

Unlike an American university with dormitories, dining halls and fixed curriculum, the École was a place where students could attend classes in required subjects, and, under the "atelier" system, receive training in design under recognized leaders in the profession. These men were generally practicing architects, rather than full time professors as such.

In design, the requirements for the degree or "Diplôme" were based on accumulating the required number of points, quickly or slowly depending on the grade or rank of the individual projects submitted in the competitive design projects. The student could take as long as he wished up to the age of thirty. He was free to work in offices to earn his living as he went along and was responsible for his own board and lodging. Compared with the development of the American university, the system was burdened with far less overhead and capital investment in buildings, and left a freer life to the student. If the architectural student took a long time getting through, he was also gaining practical experience working in offices as he went along. The system gave the student a sound education in the principles of good design: logical planning, good proportions, unity and balance—in an inspiring atmosphere. There were also examinations in practical and technical subjects for the "diplôme."

With their recognized professional education and the acclaim that attended these students returning from Paris, it was not surprising that they soon dominated the field of architecture in the United States, particularly in the East, the source of capital and the residence of the leading men of wealth and influence.

If Frick and Morgan symbolized the names of the wealthy influential patrons of these returning architects, Carrère and Hastings, and McKim, Mead and White are good examples of firms of architects who came into prominence and success under their patronage. The new "barons" accumulated the wealth and power to live in any surroundings they desired, and many wished to bring to a "backward" America an appreciation of the best in European art and culture, as they saw it. To this country they brought not only the well known collections of books and pictures but also a renaissance of classic architecture in the magnificent buildings designed by their architects to house them. It was not a time for an expression of a new architecture in a great republic but, in the words of McKim in 1897, as recorded by H. Siddon Mowbray, a time for American architecture "to catch up rather than prematurely create."

As with the start of the Renaissance in Europe at an earlier period, this was not thought of as a period of slavish copying of the works of the masters, but of bringing home an appreciation of a greater culture. America was a wide open field of opportunity and the excitement was great. Many well designed and beautiful buildings resulted which expressed the life and ideals of their patrons. They were buildings of originality in their adaptation of the classic manner; it was considered all the better if the prototype could be recognized.

Any architecture is an expression of the thinking of its times, and, providing it is well done it means little to the average person in the street whether it is labeled eclectic or modern. And the average architect of the period was happy and perfectly sincere in developing his design from a prototype. The old Savoy Plaza in New York by McKim, Mead and White was a successful adaptation of Renaissance architecture to a high building, and the expression of the soaring lines of the Woolworth Building in Gothic was a good and satisfactory solution to the design of a tall building.

In America, the graduates of the École banded together in the Society of Beaux Arts Architects and established the BAID or Beaux Arts Institute of Design. Through their efforts a basic methodology and curriculum were established in practically all the coming architectural schools in the United States.

Turning from education to the impression the new architecture made on the American public, the triumph of this "classic" architecture, far beyond the influence of work done for wealthy patrons, was the Chicago

World's Fair of 1893 entitled "The Century of Progress." Visitors from all over the United States, impressed by the unity and the sense of order in the gleaming white architectural colonnades, the uniform cornice heights, focal points monumentally expressed by great domes, the noble vistas with fountains and sculptures—carried the message to every corner of America. Public squares and buildings all over the country were built in the new image. The message was circumscribed as it was powerful, and only one local architect, whose appreciation by history was to come much later, Louis Sullivan of Chicago, was prophetic enough to say of the Fair that it would "hold back the progress of Architecture for half a century."

From the point of view of the development of a truly American architecture Sullivan was quite right, but at the moment the Beaux Arts style was the architecture in America. It meant little that people like Louis Sullivan had ideas; the architects with the Beaux Arts point of view got the jobs. Louis Sullivan almost starved from lack of work and his most famous pupil, Frank Lloyd Wright, was all but eclipsed. Wright's works, however, were published in Germany in 1912 and achieved a wide circulation, becoming a source of inspiration to many European architects, particularly in Holland.

The skyscraper itself was considered America's unique contribution to architecture, and the competition epitomized a stage in its development which, interestingly enough, began in Chicago. But it cannot be said that the skyscraper was invented in Chicago. Many essential elements awaited the time and place to be pulled together, and Chicago provided the opportunity, and the incentive. There were several reasons for this, the first being the Great Chicago Fire of 1871. It cleared the ground and created a tremendous demand for new buildings as well as encouraging new and faster methods for putting them up. The next was the development of the "Loop" district, which was created by the circuit of tracks of the suburban railroads, an internal restriction just as Chicago's external boundaries were Lake Michigan and the Chicago River. It was in the Loop that the big business district of Chicago developed, requiring higher buildings as it crowded its boundaries.

At the time, however, there was a practical limit to the height that masonry wall-bearing structures could be built. And there were just so many flights of stairs that one could climb in a day and still have time to work. Heavier buildings would sink in the mud on which Chicago was built, unlike New York City which was built on the proverbial rock. There were answers to these problems waiting to be used. For the many years before the skyscraper developed the church steeple dominated the American skyline, but some towns had shot-towers, tall structures where hot lead at the top was poured through sieves, congealing on the way down into droplets of various sizes from bird to buck shot before cooling in a tank of water at the bottom. In 1855 a shot-tower was built in New York at Broome and Centre Streets by James Bogardus, unique in that it was built with an iron frame which supported the enclosing walls.

This design of Bogardus developed rapidly into a complete building framed in iron with cast-iron fronts, often in an imitation of contemporary stone buildings and painted to resemble them. Not only were these buildings lighter in weight than the conventional wall-bearing building, but also permitted the use of more glass for light than was possible with ordinary walls. Of interest today, when new methods are receiving so much attention, these buildings were prefabricated and were shipped to all parts of the world for speedy erection.

The implications of the new type of construction were tremendous: up to this time, floors of masonry buildings were supported on walls and columns or piers, and the higher the buildings the thicker the walls and interior supports and the smaller the openings near the bottom. This meant less light and usable space where it was generally needed the most The new type of building would seem to have been the answer except for one serious shortcoming spotlighted by the Chicago fire: the failure of cast iron under great heat. Not only was it subject to cracking when water was played on it by the firemen, but some of it even melted away in the heat of the conflagration.

It is not surprising, therefore, that the next step took place in Chicago. In the iron framed Home Insurance Company Building of 1884–1885 designed by William LeBaron Jenney, the top stories were framed in a new structural material—Bessemer steel, first made in America as early as 1865. Fireproofed with masonry, steel now provided a fireproof structural material for building. Within two or three years Jenney designed a complete building framed with a cage of steel, and in 1889 Holabird and Root erected the Tacoma Building in which all the principles of framing the future skyscraper were developed for the first time. Thomas' open-hearth process of 1898 made possible the quantity production of steel, and by 1894 the catalog of the Carnegie-Phipps Co. of Pittsburgh showed standard shapes of rolled structural steel.

From now on, the open grid of steel silhouetted against the sky would be the symbol of building in the American city. With lighter weight building possible and the invention of the raft foundation to float them on the mud, buildings shot up to new levels. Eventually caisson foundations made any height possible in Chicago. With a framework in which to hang them, other important elements of the skyscraper rapidly found their place. In

67

1855 Otis demonstrated a safe elevator and in 1857 the first one was installed in the Haughwout Building at Broome Street and Broadway in New York. The first successful electric elevator was ready by 1889 and the escalator in 1900. More inventions were Edison's electric light in 1879, and Nikola Tesla's patent of the alternating current in 1888, an idea which Edison had turned down. Also in 1888, the revolving door was invented by Theophilus Van Kannel of Philadelphia.

As buildings grew higher the induced draft made it almost impossible to open the front door. Though originally invented as a "storm door," the revolving door was the answer to this problem and later became a useful device to keep the cold air from escaping through the entrances of air conditioned buildings. In 1889 reinforced concrete was used by Ernest L. Ransome in the California Academy of Sciences Building in San Francisco, and the problem of how to make plumbing and heating function in tall buildings quickly uncovered the requisite engineering talent. Following Morse's telegraph, Alexander Graham Bell invented the telephone, and the first long distance telephone was put to use in 1884. The use of gas for illumination was prolonged by the invention of the Welsbach Mantle, but the electrically lighted *auditorium* of the Auditorium Building in Chicago, 1887–1889, designed by Sullivan, showed the day of gas was over. With the Chicago Fair of 1893, the whole country was awakened to the possibilities of the new medium that had made a fairyland of the Fair at night.

By the turn of the century, the widespread usage of both the electric light and the telephone was in full swing, as well as of reinforced concrete, for floors and foundations. The skyscraper was on its way to becoming "the machine for business." With so many technical developments, architects were at first unaware that a new form was evolving, the American Skyscraper, a form which would call for an aesthetic expression of its own. Far into the next century, the frame of the skyscraper was to be cloaked in classical style—sometimes successfully adapted, to be sure.

If awareness of the new opportunities should be credited to any one architect, it should be Louis Sullivan of Chicago, whose elements for design for the framed building can be seen in the Carson-Pirie-Scott Department Store in Chicago, 1899–1904, and the Wainwright Building of St. Louis in 1891. Again in the Guaranty Building in Buffalo in 1895 we find Sullivan well on the road to finding the expression of a steel frame building with its framework encased in protective masonry against fire, and with the balance of the opening available for the use of glass. All this was part of what is now recognized historically as the Chicago School of Architecture. At the time, however, it was submerged under the weight of the Beaux Arts styles. While not necessarily the prototype, this local theory continued to develop in Europe, coming back to America after the Great Depression of 1929, as "the way to do."

The limit for wall-bearing buildings was sixteen stories, and the Monadnock Building by Burnham and Root, Chicago 1891, was the last of them, with walls seven feet thick at the bottom. With the new steel frame construction there was almost no practical limit in height, and as early as 1888 they were building the Pulitzer Building of George P. Post, 349 feet high in New York, to be followed in 1911–1913 by the Woolworth Building of Cass Gilbert, 777 feet high.

Regardless of how it was cloaked the skyscraper, as a type of structure, surged ahead, becoming the tool and symbol of big business. In grandiose, imposing and often extravagant design, it was used as a symbol to express the pride and power of great corporations. Trained in the Beaux Arts, enthusiastic member of the B.A.I.D., with experience in traditional designs and practice gained in the leading offices of the day, Raymond Hood stood on the threshold of a new era.

The Black and Gold Building

Raymond Hood's first opportunity to show the path he would take came in New York with the design of the building for the American Radiator Company at 40 West 40th Street. The lot was small, and, if the example of the other buildings in the vicinity were to be followed, this would be another typical office building sixteen or twenty stories high, with the side walls on the lot lines plain brick, on the assumption they would be hidden sooner or later by similar buildings on either side. Facing on the rear yard, the back of the building would also be plain brick, but full of windows. Only on the street facade would an effort be made to have a pleasing design with good materials.

Across the street from the building site however, was a large open space, Bryant Park. With this as a foreground one could stand back and view any structure facing thereon from top to bottom. This would not have been possible from just across a narrow street; here was a chance to do something distinctive. Raymond Hood envisaged a tower, a building designed to be seen from all sides, not just the front, and if a building twenty stories high would hardly be a skyscraper, at least there could be the illusion of one.

The sides were pinched in to create "light" courts on which windows could be located, and the two corners on the street were beveled to help create a shaft like effect. While not obvious on the exterior, a structural detail resulted that became very much a part of modern design in the era of steel and glass buildings that was to follow after the Depression. In traditional or classical buildings it was a custom to make the corner pier wider than those between the windows on the theory that it gave an illusion of strength, but the steel column in the corner actually carries only half the floor load of a column in the piers between. In beveling the corner Raymond Hood went one step further and eliminated the structural column entirely: the piece of floor that supported the three windows and their piers that rounded out two corners of the building were cantilevered out, like a shelf, from the next two columns on either side.

In later years, when the design called for all glass corners, to give an appearance of lightness and transparency to buildings, this same idea of construction was used. In the nineteen twenties, however, architects were still designing buildings to look as if they were built of solid masonry whereas, since their early development in Chicago in the 1890's high buildings were constructed with steel frames on which the relatively thin masonry exteriors were hung as a veneer.

Raymond Hood was no exception and his American Radiator Building was designed to look solid or "massive" terminating in a "silhouette" in the romantic vein of this style. To Hood, however, there seemed one false note: whereas an old fashioned tower on a castle or church might well have solid walls characterized by few openings, the requirements of offices in their modern adaptations for windows punched the fabric of these exteriors full of holes, and the towers began to look anything but solid.

To overcome this, Hood had another idea: if the black windows punched the relatively light colored masonry exterior full of holes, the thing to do was to make the walls black so the windows wouldn't show. In Mr. Hood's own words, "it was to prevent undue contrast for the countless windows in what might destroy the mass silhouette."

So the building was faced with black brick. For Hood's desired effect nobody should work after hours, and as Dr. Creese has pointed out, it was left to Georgia O'Keefe to make a painting of the building at night with all the lights turned on—still a fabric punched full of holes.

The top of the building was properly finished with a silhouette well modeled in order to be seen in equally pleasing detail from all sides, wherever it could be seen against the sky. The effect of a tower had been achieved, and there was room for one more idea at the top. The use of floodlights on billboards for advertising at night was already established: why not gild the top of the black building for effect by day and then floodlight it by night, utilizing the building as a billboard for itself? The owner agreed. For a company selling furnaces and heaters, a building that glowed in the dark like a torch was not such a wild idea.

(opposite page) The black and gold building—American Radiator Building.

courtesy of the author

American Radiator Building at night. *courtesy of Samuel H. Gottscho*

Long after the building was under construction, Raymond Hood was still coming up with ideas. One draftsman told me he was actually sent over to the job to measure steel already in place, to see if one more change would be possible before it was too late. The building was finished in 1924, and was in later years designated by the New York Landmarks Commission. A tablet placed on the building reads:

LANDMARKS OF NEW YORK
AMERICAN-STANDARD BUILDING
Raymond M. Hood's use of black brick trimmed with gold colored stone, in the design of this building, is an early instance of vivid coloration on the surface of a skyscraper. Construction was completed in 1924 for the American Radiator Company, organized in 1892. Plaque erected 1962 by the New York Community Trust.

72

Boom Times

On completion of the American Radiator Building, Raymond Hood moved his office to the fourteenth floor of the building. Here, besides the general and private offices, there was a drafting room large enough for twelve or fourteen men. Since the early twenties, Hood's partner had been J. André Fouilhoux, a French engineer trained in Paris. A tall, quiet gentleman of the old school, Fouilhoux' slow and thoughtful demeanor was in quite a contrast to the effervescence of his short and excitable partner.

It was a good combination. Mr. Fouilhoux contributed an analytical mind and was one to withhold his answers until he had thought them through, rather than seemingly to rely on a flash of intuition. On the many difficult practical problems that would arise his answers were waited for and listened to with respect. Above all, I remember Fouilhoux for his ever courteous and considerate manner towards all with whom he had dealings, and under all circumstances.

In 1924, Hood and Fouilhoux were joined by Frederick A. Godley, and the partnership was now called Raymond Hood, Godley and Fouilhoux. Godley had a wide acquaintance and was well liked. In the office he generally carried out the projects of his own clients rather than participating in those of Raymond Hood. Godley retired in 1931 to become a professor at the Yale School of Architecture.

By this time Raymond Hood could begin to look back on quite a bit of accomplished work since winning the *Tribune* Competition. With Fouilhoux he had designed the St. Vincent de Paul Asylum in Tarrytown, completed in 1924. For Mr. and Mrs. William R. Morris, Hood designed a charming home in Greenwich, Connecticut, at the time of their marriage. They were close friends of his and became frequent visitors to the home he was to build for himself and family nearby on Southfield Point in Stamford. Of these days, Mrs. Morris recalls that their favorite cocktail, served like as not after a game of tennis, was applejack, lemon juice and absinthe.

Hood's own home was a comfortable and pleasant house of stucco and fieldstone, with no pretentions as to modern architecture. The site was on the water with enough land for the various recreational activities in which Hood was interested. While his friends in New York may not have realized it, he was quite an athlete and a very good tennis player. Hood had his own tennis court, and plenty of space for other games. There was even a dock for the cabin cruiser he had acquired.

Hood's sons remember that one afternoon a man came to see them about going to a boys' camp for the summer, telling about the many things they

Residence of Mr. and Mrs. William R. Morris, Greenwich, Conn.

courtesy of McGraw-Hill

St. Vincent de Paul Asylum, Tarrytown, by Hood and Fouilhoux.

courtesy of Hood family

Residence of Raymond Hood, Stamford, Conn.   *courtesy of McGraw-Hill*

could do there: swimming, boating, tennis, ball games and many other enjoyable activities. Richard and Raymond, Jr., replied that it all sounded like good fun but they didn't see why they should go away to camp when they could do all the same things right at home.

When I visited the Hoods' one weekend, I noticed one architectural detail. After graduating from school, a young architect is expected to gain some practical experience in an office, and one of the things impressed upon me by one patient tutor before I left Boston was that one should never have a change of levels in a building with only one step between, always two or more.

I saw the truth of the admonition with my own eyes as the boys raced across the living room to greet their father, only to fall flat on their faces. Even in their own home, a one step difference in the middle of the floor was a hazard.

75

According to the children, their father was inordinately fond of fire-crackers and salutes, lighting them while he held them in his fingers. Inclined to be a little absent minded, it was a miracle he didn't blow his fingers off. Most of all, his children remember him as a builder and flier of wonderful kites.

That Sunday, we had lunch on the yacht. Mrs. Hood asked who would like to be the cook and, as the lad from the office, I volunteered. Dropping down through the hatch into the little galley, I soon had the small steaks on the griddle. In those days, my idea of a steak was something well done, and when I had cooked them to a turn, I passed them up through the hatch, pleased with my effort. I joined the others on the deck, in blissful ignorance until much later.

Hood's further work included winning the competition for the Masonic Temple and Scottish Rite Cathedral, which was built in Scranton, Pennsylvania in 1929. A sequel to the American Radiator Building was the designing of the National Radiator Building in London, which also had a black exterior. Hood's English associate was J. Gordon Reeves.

National Radiator Building, London.

courtesy of McGraw-Hill

Raymond Hood at home, Stamford, Conn.   *courtesy of Gottscho-Schleisner, Inc.*

While Raymond Hood had other interests besides the work of his office, his love of architecture for its own sake ran through them all. He was devoted to the old Beaux Arts Institute of Design, founded by graduates of the École des Beaux Arts in Paris for the purpose of advancing architectural design in this country. The Society was largely made up of practicing architects, not necessarily graduates of the École des Beaux Arts, who, in various committees, prepared programs for competitive architectural design projects to be used in the various architectural schools and ateliers. In return, the schools joined the society together with their students, receiving the programs for use in their design courses.

Ateliers were places where draftsmen working in offices during the day could work at night on the design projects under the guidance of some leading architect who volunteered his time. The draftsmen would earn credits in the B.A.I.D. for this design work which would help them in meeting the requirements for becoming registered architects in the states later on.

The programs were issued on time to meet the scheduled curricula of the schools and had definite dates for return of the drawings to the Society's headquarters. Here juries of local architects were organized, which judged the work of the students and gave out relative grades, sometimes with a real prize or a medal. Some projects were funded so the winners could travel, or in the case of the highest award, the Paris Prize, attend the Beaux Arts itself. Competition was keen and the rivalry between the schools for awards was great.

It is of interest in our biography that in 1919 the program for the final competition for the Twelfth Paris Prize of the Society of Beaux Arts Architects was written by Raymond Hood. The title was, *The Capital Building of the League of Nations.* The competition was won by Ernest E. Weihe, who later became a well-known architect in San Francisco.

The considered advantage of the system was that practicing architects prepared the programs and judged the results, so that the student could feel he was up against a more real and broader world than if the programs had been prepared and judged only by the faculty of his school. He was also being judged by the people with whom he might later want a job. On the other hand, the architects themselves were keeping up with the spirit of the times, making acquaintances, in name at least, of upcoming graduates of ability whom they might like to employ later on.

Raymond Hood was a keen participant in the juries and devoted much of his time to them, but not, I am told, without his contrary side showing up occasionally. Perhaps after a long hard session of reviewing drawings, eliminating the weaker and moving the stronger on ahead, the jury would have reached the point of voting on the prize awards and first places in the

peculiar Beaux Arts nomenclature.

About this time Raymond Hood would evince some doubt whether they were quite ready. "I am just wondering," he would say, "whether we gave that young fellow a fair shake."

He would go way back through the pile to some drawing eliminated in the beginning and bring it to the front, while the jury by this time would be sitting on chairs with drawings on easels in front of them. Hood would begin talking up the good points of the drawing he had fished out, somehow or other not realized before. If he could talk that drawing all the way up to a first place, his evening was made.

One older participant in these juries was John Mead Howells. Some believe that it was on occasions when they were on juries together that Howells became favorably impressed with the abilities of the younger Raymond Hood. This could explain why, when the time came, Howells was to invite Hood to be his partner in the *Chicago Tribune*.

Another version, quoted from the book, *The News,* 1968, is this:

"Hood, at the time, was out of a job and had a sick wife. One day walking through Grand Central Terminal in New York, he met John Mead Howells who had been a classmate at the Beaux Arts in Paris. Howells, of an old Boston family, had the means and connections to open his own office and had done very well. Hood, without money or status, had worked for a number of architects. That day he congratulated Howells on his invitation to enter the *Tribune* competition. Howells said his shop was so busy that he couldn't accept the invitation. After they parted, Howells turned on his heel, called out to Hood and brought him back. He suggested that Hood, if he were interested, could use his office to work on the Tribune Tower plan, and keep the fee—which was a godsend at the time.

The "Four-Hour Lunch Club" that met at Mori's Restaurant on Fridays was almost an institution. In addition to Raymond Hood there was his closest friend, Joseph Urban, a Viennese architect who had come to New York, initially achieving success as a designer of sets for the Metropolitan Opera. He finally had the opportunity he wanted to design buildings as well, perhaps through people he met at the luncheons.

Urban's best known buildings were the Ziegfeld Theater and the New School for Social Research. Ely Jacques Kahn was also a regular member, and Ralph Walker frequently joined them. They are said to have tuned up on a cocktail dubbed "Nipple Spray" by Urban, followed by crab flake pancakes with cheese sauce, prepared by Mori's best Italian cook. There were nearly always guests, like Tony Sarg, the artist, Frank Lloyd Wright, as Ely Jacques Kahn described him, "damned positive about everything," and

Architectural League Dinner.   *courtesy of Empire*

Alvin Johnson. The group was not limited to artists and architects; from time to time there might be found someone like Dr. John H. Finley, a distinguished editor of the *New York Times*. He was especially noted for giving a medal each year for some feat of walking, such as a circuit of Manhattan, or the greatest mileage chalked up in a day around the tables by a waiter with a pedometer.

I met Dr. Finley in 1928 and recall his telling me of his current award. "This year," he said, "I gave my medal to Charles Augustus Lindbergh. Not that his feat was one of walking, but still, I think he deserved it."

Raymond Hood's favorite gathering place was probably the old Architectural League on East Fortieth, the same street as his office and not far from the corner of Park Ave. Two old houses had been combined to make a headquarters for the League, including a dining room. It shared its roof with a number of smaller societies and offices such as the B.A.I.D., the Municipal Art Society of New York, the New York Chapter of the A.I.A. and the Fine Arts Federation of New York. For architects, painters, sculptors and others with related interests in the building field, the League was a focal point. Here, those interested in the excitement of a dynamic world of architectural activity and progress could exchange their ideas.

The "Three Little Napoleons of Architecture," as they were known, Raymond Hood, Ely Kahn and Ralph Walker, were usually there at lunch time, marking up many a table cloth between them with soft pencils. Among other friends of Raymond Hood to be seen there were Ken Murchison and George Chappel, and both full of fun and stories. There were also Putnam Brinley, Lee Lawrie and Archie (Archibald Manning) Brown.

A special group of artists or "delineators" who made the final perspective renderings of many of the architects' projects, were also members. The drawings were for the purpose of showing the client what his building would look like, or for publicity. The talents of Hugh Ferris, Schell Lewis and Chester Price were in great demand, those of Hugh Ferris especially for his romantic illusionary visions of the city. Schell Lewis and Chester Price were greatly admired for their facility with a pencil depicting the subtle texture of buildings and settings of beautiful trees, an art that seemed to be dying out as the air brush gradually became the medium for such pictures.

It was said all three of these men were born in St. Louis and swam in the same creek, which somehow accounted for their native talent. I had a chance to question Schell Lewis about this when in his eighties and still at work. He said no, it wasn't exactly true and only one of them had been born in St. Louis. However, it was true that at one time or another they had all gone swimming in the same creek, long since buried, I fear, in huge drain pipes under the expanding city. Future artists in this field, I guess, will have to learn the hard way and go to school.

Ely Jacques Kahn, by Tony Sarg, '31
courtesy of S.B.A.A.

Self-portrait by Tony Sarg, '31.
courtesy of S.B.A.A.

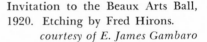
Invitation to the Beaux Arts Ball,
1920. Etching by Fred Hirons.
courtesy of E. James Gambaro

The artistic and architectural social event of the year was the annual Beaux Arts Ball at the Astor Hotel, now demolished, one of New York's big events, and perhaps the wettest, since it was during Prohibition. Many an idea for the Ball was hatched and developed at the Architectural League. Each ball had a theme; one year it was the New York skyline. In that pageant the leading architects paraded in costumes symbolizing the skyscrapers they had designed, complete with electric lights that twinkled in the windows of the hollow models they wore on their heads.

In 1928 the subject of the Ball, destined to be one of the last, was "The French Occupation of North Africa." As one of the student class of the B.A.I.D. who worked daytimes in the various architects' offices I helped paint scenery for the Ball, and like the other collaborators was rewarded with a ticket to the Ball. A pair of pajamas with red bottoms and a black top seemed to provide an adequate impression of a French costume. I rented an immense red wig for the occasion, for three dollars. Mr. Reinhard kindly gave me a seat at a table, and at practically no cost I was all set for the most expensive party in New York.

In order that guests have the freedom of the various rooms of the hotel and to avoid a constant exchange of "rain checks," the back of the hand of each guest was rubber stamped with a special insignia indicating he had pre-

Group photo of the Beaux Arts Ball Committee of 1927, including Raymond Hood.

courtesy of Underwood and Underwood

(*back row—left to right*) C. B. Falls, John "Ted" Haneman, George S. Chappell, G. Putnam Brinley, Benjamin Wistar Morris, James W. O'Connor, Harry Allen Jacobs, Harry R. Burt, Tony Sarg, Clinton Mackenzie, Edward S. Hewitt, John E. Sheridan.

(*center row*) (Harry) Oothout Milliken, Julian Clarence Levi, James Monroe Hewlett, Arthur Ware, Kenneth M. Murchison, *Chairman*, John D. Boyd, Edward McCarten, Joseph H. Freedlander.

(*front row*) Henry (Harry) Renwick Segwick, Raymond Mathewson Hood, James Reynolds, Whitney Warren, *Honorary Chairman* (Born: Jan. 1864, Died: Jan. 24, 1943).

THE COMMITTEE FOR THE BEAUX-ARTS BALL—Held at the Hotel Astor, New York City, Broadway & West 44th Street, on January 27, 1928.
Sponsored by The Society of Beaux-Arts Architects.
Ball Theme: "The French Occupation of Northern Africa"—1847.
Photograph taken at the home of Whitney Warren during November 1927.

SBAA disbanded 1941—all members assigned to the Beaux Arts Institute of Design and name BAID now known as National Institute for Architectural Education, 20 West 40th Street, New York, N.Y. 10018. MU 4-1948 (name changed June 29, 1956)

sented his ticket at the door. The other young lads in the various offices who wanted to come too thought this was a very good idea; by pre-arrangement one of the first to get to the ball with a ticket would leave and head for the nearest office. There the design was carefully copied onto a blank rubber stamp, to be engraved thereon by another lad handy with tools. The hands of all those waiting to get in free were properly stamped and off they went.

For a short time I experienced that singular freedom from inhibition that such an event demands, since I was lost behind my wig and felt no one could possibly recognize me.

On the way up the grand staircase I met a beautiful lady in a gorgeous costume, and like nearly everybody else, weaving slightly in spirit-induced euphoria. As I approached, she slowly waved a finger in my face as if seeking to recognize me. Then it came, "I remember you, you're the man who burned the steaks." So faded my memory of a happy weekend with the boss. The lady was Mrs. Hood.

One of the members of the League was Howard Greenley, a graduate of the Beaux Arts in Paris, and a great raconteur. One of his stories was about himself as a young man returning from Paris to his home town in Bayonne, New Jersey. At this time the area was the center of the terra cotta industry. Glazed terra cotta, particularly, had developed into a most useful material on the exterior of buildings. Whether for structural or ornamental purpose it was shaped while in the plastic state of clay and then baked into a most durable weather resisting material. The Woolworth Building is a great example of its use.

The ornamental work was limited only by the sculptural talents of the artisan in following out the designs of the architect, and Howard Greenley's father was one of these skillful artisans. His son was to take the next step up the ladder and become an architect, and ways and means were found to send the boy to the École des Beaux Arts in Paris.

When Greenley returned several years later, he was a polished young man, speaking French beautifully, and an "Architecte Diplômé par le Gouvernement Français." The whole town shared in the family pride, and more than that they wanted to give this distinguished young man a good start. In those horse and buggy days, it was decided a most suitable project would be the design of a great public fountain in the main square, which would include a basin for watering tired and thirsty horses. The fountain itself would be built of terra cotta in recognition of the home industry.

The young man worked hard on his first commission, and the Committee, including the Mayor, was more than pleased with the results. A great celebration was planned for the unveiling, and it seemed appropriate that this unveiling of the fountain be accompanied by a demonstration of its purpose. As part of the parade, it was arranged to obtain from the Anheuser-Busch Company their finest dray, complete with beer barrels and drawn by a magnificent team of Clydesdales.

The multitude assembled, the band played, and speeches followed. Our young hero accepted the accolade to the blare of trumpets as the veil was lifted. The pavement began to tremble as down the main avenue came the great team of horses at a full gallop. High in the seat the driver cracked his long whip. It was a magnificent spectacle as the team neared the fountain that gleamed in the sun, splashing with water. With all the skill of an excellent driver, he reined in his horses at the last possible moment. But he had forgotten one thing. The horses were hitched to the wagon by a long center pole, and as the horses pulled back in the breeching at the very edge of the fountain, the pole, driven by the wagon's momentum, shot forward with all the force of a battering ram.

From dedication to demolition, probably no architectural monument in history ever had a shorter life. The young man's father said, "Well, son," as he kicked aside a few shattered fragments, "I guess that's that."

New Limits and New Horizons

In 1916 New York City passed a new Zoning Ordinance, as we mentioned in the beginning of the book. Until then a property owner had been relatively free to crowd as much building on his site as he could, and to build as high as he wanted with no obligation to consider the effect on neighboring properties. If his structure should block the light of that of an adjacent owner, someone else in turn might still do the same thing to him a year or two later.

With the tendency of big business to come together with their offices in one mutually convenient area, the Wall Street district became the supreme example of what this "laissez faire" policy could do. The enormous office buildings, vast ant hills of human beings piled high on the narrow streets, created dim canyons where the sunlight hardly penetrated. And in those days before air conditioning and modern lighting, buildings counted on their windows for daylight and ventilation. Finally, the ever worsening conditions were recognized as serious.

To provide for better building conditions to remedy the situation, a new law was devised. One fundamental requirement presumed a line representing the minimum desired angle of light, sloping back from the center of the street; the facade of a building could rise vertically until the line of the roof or cornice intersected this line. Additional stories above this height would have to be set back to stay within the line. And for buildings not

85

running all the way through the block, rear yards were required, also with a setback provision as they increased in height. There had to be courts on the sides of buildings to permit windows.

When the area at any level had been reduced to twenty-five percent of the lot due to the effect of the set-backs on all sides, then the building could continue straight up to unlimited heights without further reduction in area. It was this last provision that was of especial interest to skyscraper builders, as we saw in the first two chapters of this book.

Hitherto, architects had been guided by the classic principles of design and proportions as they were taught at the École des Beaux Arts. Reference to a historical prototype often influenced the details of their designs. An example of such classic treatment of a tall building is the New York City Municipal Building by McKim, Mead and White. Although the exterior walls are hung on the steel frame the details of the design are inspired by architecture of wall-bearing structures from the time of the Romans.

With the new law the architect's first consideration in his design had to be a literal interpretation of the regulations, not a reference to the traditions of the past. At first it did not occur to them that this would mean the old ways should be discarded and new details and proportions developed that would be compatible with the new regulations. The architect instead tried to bend the traditional ways into conformity with the new.

The Heckscher Building on Fifth Avenue was the first of the tall buildings to be constructed under the new law. Faced with observing the new rules of setbacks, dormers, and restricted area towers, all new elements, the wonder of the Heckscher Building's design is that the architect was able to observe them all and still emerge with the same old kind of building. George Harold Edgell, the Dean of the Harvard Architectural School, in his *History of Architecture* says:

> "In this case the designer using details of the early French Renaissance has been forced to conform in mass to the envelope prescribed by law. As a result, the building is designed in receding blocks and finally crowned with a tower. It is an imposing pile, although not wholly successful, with the horizontals overemphasized and there is nothing to bind any of the masses to those above or below."

The building was topped off by a Gaelic cock.

Things were stirring nonetheless. The imaginative studies of Hugh Ferris in visualizing the city of the future, its forms moulded by the requirements of the new law, stimulated the searching for a new expression in architecture. Ferris' pictures were an inspiration not only to architects but to their clients as well. To open "the eyes that do not see and the ears that do not hear," Le Corbusier sounded the three trumpet calls of architecture:

(*Left*) A. Heckscher Building, Fifth Ave., New York, by Whitney Warren. First tower building designed under new law. Classic style in new mold.

(*Right*) B. Shelton Hotel, Lexington, Ave., by Arthur Loomis Harmon. New forms of Zoning Law recognized in architecture.   *courtesy of the author*

mass, surface, plan. In these criteria for the time a new movement could be detected.

In mass, the Heckscher Building was a rather disorganized pile of boxes lacking in harmonious design. Arthur Loomis Harmon, another architect, recognized the new problem and undertook to see what he could do about composing the "pile of boxes." The result may be seen in the Shelton Hotel, where the cubical shapes were developed from requirements of the zoning law into a very satisfactory composition. In the overall effect, any recall of details from an earlier period are unnoticed.

Ralph Walker successfully carried the principles of design in mass still further with an irregular site and one that could be seen from the river, the Barclay-Vesey Telephone Building on Vesey Street in Lower Manhattan. Walker also worked out his own details rather than relying on traditional forms.

When we think of the second consideration, surface, the name of Ely Kahn comes back to mind. Kahn designed a great many of the loft buildings of the period. Unlike the skyscraper with its tower, the loft building was designed to obtain the greatest floor areas possible, generally for light manufacturing purposes. The distance from the windows was not thought to matter, nor was it advisable to go above these floors into small set back or tower floors. Ely Kahn concentrated on interesting treatment of the surface of the building, developing ornamental detail, often in geometric patterns, to give light, shade, and often color effects. The bold use of colored terra cotta around the top can be seen in the building at Number Two Park Avenue, and the details in the entrance lobby were some of the best modern designs of the day.

On the narrow streets like those in the Wall Street district, where buildings could be seen only from a short distance, this concern with detail was important. The mass became of greater consideration when the building could be seen from a distance, and as Raymond Hood said, to worry about the details of something as huge as a modern office building is like wondering what sort of a lace shawl you should hang on an elephant.

(*Left*) C. Prince John and Gold St. Building, No. 2 Park Ave., by Ely Jacques Kahn. A new surface treatment of large masses with color and decoration. (*Right*) D. Fred F. French Building, Fifth Ave., New York. Example of transition from set-backs to tower under new zoning law.   *courtesy of the author*

In the plan, the third of Le Corbusier's criteria, lies the greatest interest. As he himself said, "The plan necessitates the most active imagination . . . severe discipline . . . and austere abstraction." The Zoning Law not only made planning much more interesting for high buildings but more difficult. The architect could no longer think of a typical plan that would carry as high as he wanted to build: he had to begin at the ground with the plan that was flexible enough to adapt itself to the changing shapes above that were caused by the setbacks and dormers.

With the construction boom in New York, every building entered a competition. Every inch of space possible had to produce rent, and the manner in which space was arranged in the building with reference to light and air determined its value. Offices and hotels required a limited depth space from the windows, and this meant designing so that the space above was not too deep below the setbacks or too shallow.

Elevator shafts were of necessity a strictly vertical element, but it was no longer possible to assume an ideal lower floor plan for them. In a high building the elevator shafts must also give a good floor plan in the tower where area and the possibilities were limited. The tower brought the highest rent, but it also cost the most to build. In the higher buildings the first bank of elevators might run to the fifteenth floor, a second bank to the thirtieth, and a third to the forty-fifth. If not carefully worked out, the first bank and then the second would stop off, leaving a dark space in the plans far back from the windows. The high rent of the tower was paid for space with windows, naturally, not dark space.

It was consideration of factors like these that emphasized the three-dimensional aspect of planning. This of course was before the days of air conditioning, or the acceptance or even practicality of "all glass" buildings. It was still the era of saving old newspapers and string, and the emphasis was on getting the maximum amount of building for the least cost. Land values were skyrocketing, and the building costs were expensive compared to other items in the economy. In the twenties occurred the great movement to the cities, and the growth of the skyscraper witnessed not only the increase in congestion but the development of the building as a machine for more efficient business. The skyscraper pinpointed this concentration and became the distribution point of all types of financial, intellectual and physical exchange, all dependent on improved communications.

It was probably not the implications of the Zoning Law as such that excited Raymond Hood, in the case of the *Daily News* Building, but the challenge of designing a successful skyscraper within its limitations and expressive of those limitations. These were not necessarily a handicap, for, as it has often been said, architecture begins with the establishing of limits. *89*

"City of Towers" model for New York by Raymond Hood, showing development of towers and demolition of low buildings in between to give city of towers with plenty of ground area. *courtesy of the author*

But Hood was excited about the details of working out a successful plan, like finding the solution to a puzzle.

Once a satisfying scheme was reached, its expression in the mass appearance or effect of the building became equally important, as is witnessed by Hood's use of plasticine models which could be readily modified until a satisfying form was achieved.

The details of decoration did not interest Hood especially, and this exacting work was generally left to Mr. H. V. K. Henderson of Hood's office. Mr. Henderson had definite and exacting theories on such designs, which he developed meticulously, perhaps more successfully in Gothic than in the newer forms stimulated by the Paris Exposition of 1925. Raymond Hood's palette of colors was rather limited, according to Don Hatch. When the subject of the color of something came up, Hood would be likely to say, "What color? Let's see. How many colors are there—red, yellow and blue? Let's make it red."

Raymond Hood's most absorbing interest was the place of the skyscraper as a desirable place for human activity and how it would fit into the scheme of a city. People were already talking about the idea of a city of widely separated towers, with low buildings or landscaping in between.

"Villes-Tours," a tower city, was illustrated in Le Corbusier's *Vers une Architecture* in 1924 and also in the volume *Urbanisme,* the two volumes I had with me when I first stepped into Raymond Hood's offices.

A plan like that of Le Corbusier's for his "Ville Contemporaine," or "Centre de Paris," would have meant tearing down half of the city of Paris. Raymond Hood was more practical. It seemed unreasonable to attempt to tear down half the city of New York at once and begin again from scratch with some architect's idea of what New York City should look like.

The idea could be put into practice here and there on a small scale, as opportunity offered, for little by little the old buildings would come down. It would be possible, by concentrating their replacement in skyscrapers and keeping these reasonably far apart, to attain the goal of a "city of towers." Not only was this scheme more practical but it was more humane and picturesque; there would be scattered towers of individual design rather than the rigid pattern of symmetrical buildings shown in Le Corbusier's illustrations.

And indeed the low or antiquated buildings were torn down between the modern skyscrapers, because they were no longer producing income. The Depression helped to prove the point that the idea of opening up spaces was not inconceivable. With these theories in mind, Raymond Hood in January 1928 approached the design of the *Daily News* Building. For him, at last, Gothic was to be set aside.

The Inside Story of the Daily News Building

After a noteworthy building is finished, there comes the day of the critics, which is followed by that of the architectural historians. As they are unaware of what the architect had in mind, their conjectures are often far afield from his reasoning. As time passes, the judgments of such people tend to reflect later theories of architecture, irrelevant as they may be to the period when the building was designed.

Some may be surprised that Raymond Hood did not concern himself with the question of how to express the steel columns on the exterior, or even whether they should be lost entirely behind a facade of glass. It did not occur to Hood that the vertical piers of white brick might represent extended rolls of newsprint as an expression of the purpose of the building. One editor, however, illustrated this theory by an actual photograph developed from the pattern of parallel strips of toilet paper rolled out across the carpet.

The design actually began with the mundane efforts of a stenographer struggling to open a succession of windows of various sizes. Now the Real

Estate Management consultants had determined the size of the basic unit of office space for this building as that required by one man and his desk. This came to eight feet six inches, and partitions would form individual offices of this width. Since ventilation depended on the windows and maximum use was also made of available daylight, the largest size for a practical window was important.

The typical double hung window gave the best circulation of air, because such windows could be let down from the top and raised at the bottom. There was also the advantage of weather tight construction. However, the steel of which these windows were made was heavy, and they were painted, which made them stick. They could be made any reasonable width; the question was how wide they could be and still be operated by the average office worker.

Since the age of chivalry was long past, a representative of the "weaker sex" was given the job of opening a series of windows of increasing sizes. The largest she could conveniently operate was four feet six inches wide. This left a nominal pier of four feet between windows. Under the structural system used, every other pier would face a steel column—to the critics this meant the one between was a fake. But they never looked at the plans.

Raymond Hood, in fact, was much more motivated by the logic than the theory. Buildings are full of pipes, conduits and ducts as well as steel columns. On the outside wall, it was customary to locate these utility lines on either side of the steel column, regardless of how wide it made the pier. In the case of this building, the pier would have had to be made wider than the space determined above for space between windows. Hood's solution was to locate the pipes and wires in the intervening pier, so that both the pier and the column were functional, as well as equal in width. Thus there was still a convenient arrangement of office partitions, and every office unit had a window and an equal amount of wall space on either side. This alternate arrangement of structural piers and utility piers gave the building its characteristic appearance of vertical stripes.

Captain Patterson had agreed that his building should have a tower. Characteristically, Hood thought a tower must have windows all around, if possible, with a depth of good space behind them. There was no problem about having windows looking out over the two streets and over the printing plant on the rear: but how could there be windows on the west side along the lot line of the public school? No scheme based on the courtyards of the Zoning Law seemed to give the desired results. A large amount of space would always result with no windows or, at best, undesirable windows subdivided into small panes with wire glass for fire safety.

To Raymond Hood with his dream of a city with free standing towers,

Final small scale model of *Daily News* Building in plaster.

courtesy of the author

it occurred that the problem could be solved if the owner would be willing to give up a strip of land from street to street on the plot line. Allowing for a useful depth of space facing on it, such a strip would be twenty-five feet wide. This would mean giving up a large section of space in the lower part of the building corresponding to 5000 sq.ft. of ground space for which good money had been paid. From that point of view there seemed little chance that the owner's representatives or his real estate advisors would ever agree to the idea.

Hood presented it another way. At the next meeting of the board of design he said he was bothered about some aspects of the type of space they should try to obtain in the plan. Making a diagram of the end of the site running through from 42nd to 41st Street, Hood asked their help:

"Now tell me, Mr. Landauer," he said innocently enough, "if we have windows on 42nd Street and windows on 41st Street, and a blank wall all the way down the side, nearly two hundred feet, what kind of space do you call that?"

"Why Mr. Hood, that's what we call 'loft' space," replied Landauer.

"Now Mr. Landauer, just about what is this space worth?"

"Well, Mr. Hood, that might be worth a dollar or a dollar and a half a square foot."

"Now I'm just talking through my hat, but I would like to bring up an idea here that may clear things up for me: Supposing we were to move this blank wall back from the lot line, so that we could have windows the full length of this west side here, making this space about twenty-five feet deep all the way around from 42nd Street, down the side and around 41st Street, what kind of space would you call that?"

"Well, Mr. Hood, that's what we call 'office' space."

"And what, Mr. Landauer, would that kind of space be worth?"

"That might be worth $2.75 to $3.00 a square foot, Mr. Hood."

"Now I want to get this straight," said Hood, closing the trap, "if I build half as much space, saving sixty cents a cubic foot, I can get twice as much for what is left, or the same amount as I would have for the original 'loft' space. Is that right?"

They must have realized they were being taken in by the seemingly ingenuous architect, but it made sense. They agreed to the proposal and the west side of the tower became all windows. Since then, this principle of giving up ground space to public use has been followed with many buildings.

The future *Daily News* Building now had the windows of a tower and at least a token open space on one side as well as on the streets. It would be an early member in the future city of towers. An "exchange of easements" was subsequently arranged with the City whereby, for a deed to the strip of land for use as a thoroughfare, they agreed that, at such time as the public school was demolished, the City would add an equal contiguous strip, making a full width street of fifty feet. In the interim, the *News* would have "air" rights over the school and thus there could be standard windows for light and air the full height and width of this side of the building. But getting this "exchange of easements" was not as easy as it sounded to us then. We may read of the account in *The News* written years afterwards:

"Getting the Board of Education to do anything was a formidable job. Fortunately again, *The News* had the man for the project. Clarence Worden had started as a copy boy with the Brooklyn Standard Union 14 years before, advanced by stages to reporter. He was 17 when he enlisted in the army in 1917, served in France with the 470 Aero Squadron; returned to his old job after the war. In 1924 he came to *The News* as City Hall reporter. Worden was a favorite of Mayor Walker, and president of the Inner Circle, the association of City Hall reporters, and had considerable standing with the politicians. In June 1928, he had been appointed secretary of the Board of Education: but after four months decided he was not the man for the office, and came back to *The News*. Worden was tapped to prevail upon the board to relinquish the 25 feet desired.

"He did his homework well with Hood, prepared a presentation showing that sacrificing the strip on the side of its lot was to the permanent advantage of the Board of Education Office building. The approval of 30-odd officials of the Board of Estimate, various commissioners, and officers of the Board of Education was required. Worden started with the officials he knew, got introductions and appointments with those he had not known before. And in two months secured the 30-odd letters of recommendation required. The measure to use the school property for the throughway was formally approved.

"After watching Worden's operation, Holliss concluded that he was wasted as a reporter, and made him his assistant. Worden's victory, however, proved to be pyrrhic: After the 1929 market crash, the plans for the new office building for the Board of Education went down the drain. Forty-one years later, the same old Commercial High School is still doing business at the same old stand. There is no 50-foot throughway, but *The News* still has its private 25-foot alley.'

It may be noted the city has continued the idea of a new street for two blocks south of the *News* Building helping, in this case with traffic from the Mid-Town Tunnel.

Between the top of one window and the bottom of the next one is a filler, known as a spandrel. For the spandrel design of the *Daily News* Building, Mr. Henderson worked out a progressive geometric pattern of red and black bricks to complement the severity of the white brick piers. The major facade of the *News* Building as seen from midtown would be along the new street, and it also faced west. When people began to pull down the shades against the afternoon sun, the whole effect of the related design of the piers and spandrels in vertical strips could be upset, for the curtains could be in as wide a variety of patterns and colors as there were tenants.

Before the tenants moved in, as soon as the building was up Hood had samples of various window shades sent over to the job and tried out in the windows. The final selection was made by observing from the street; red was to be used in all the window shades, avoiding the disturbing and disorderly effect of a haphazard collection of colored shades.

In the steel framing of the building, Hood made another innovation. A "wing" of the tower extended from the central elevator section toward 41st Street, about sixty feet wide allowing for a corridor down the center and rental space on either side. In framing such a wing, it was common practice to divide it into three equal structural bays. This would result in the intermediate column being in the usable space on either side of the corridor. This is the way the engineers showed it when they brought in their plan for review.

Hood pointed out that such columns would be in the way of people using the space, and if there had to be columns they should be located in a necessary wall, like that of the corridor. The engineers didn't see things that way. Anybody knew, they said, that if the space were divided into three equal bays the beams would all be the same size, cheaper to fabricate, more economical in the use of steel, and would result in the least projection into the ceiling below. In the view of the engineers it was ridiculous to consider locating two columns so close together on either side of the corridor and leave long deep spaces to the outer walls. People had always put up with columns in their work space and they might as well go on doing so.

Hardly convinced, Hood faced them with, "Listen, if you can't design the building the way I want it, I'll hire engineers who can."

The next day, Weiskopf and Pickworth returned with the solution: While it was unreasonable to have two columns so close together on either side of the corridor, there was no reason why there could not be a single column on one side of the corridor, even though it would be off center. It was true that this plan would result in unequal distances to the outside walls, but the girders could still be the same length. If the girder were made of a pair of steel beams instead of a single one, the beams could be attached on either side of the column on brackets extending by it into the center of the corridor. This short section over the corridor was called a cantilever. Another girder of paired beams of equal lengths could then hang on the ends of the cantilevers and extend to the other outside wall.

The unusual idea was good for everyone; the architect had his way and the engineers were happy with their solution. While a girder made up of one beam would have extended too far into the ceiling space below, reducing the head room, a pair of girders substantially reduced this depth. It was true that two girders of paired beams did require a greater weight of steel than the original three shorter ones, but it could be justified by the savings of the weight of a column and the cost of the connections to it all the way up through the building. The engineers were conscientious, too.

Earlier it was mentioned how Hood solved the problem of the top of the building; after the period of the embellishing of skyscrapers with pinnacles, spires, lanterns or tempietos, the square-topped simplicity of a building like the *Daily News* seemed to set the pace for others, judging by the profiles that grew up along Park Avenue. This solution was so successful that it appears even Frank Lloyd Wright would have liked the credit for it.

96

(*Opposite page*) *New York Daily News* Building before the elevated railway was torn down. *courtesy of the author*

It was many years later, after Raymond Hood had died, that I happened to be invited to sit down in a spare seat at a table where Mr. Wright was a guest for luncheon.

Mr. Wright was in the middle of a story about a time many years before when he happened to be in New York and telephoned Raymond Hood to say hello. At that time Hood was designing the *Daily News* Building. Mr. Wright was quoting himself as having said "Listen Ray, you sound worried, what's troubling you?"

"Well, I'll tell you Frank," Wright quoted Hood as saying, "I'm working on this new office building and I've got the model up to thirty-seven stories and don't know how to finish it. Would you come over to the office and help me out?"

Wright went on to describe going "over to the office to have a look. There was a plasticine model of the building with a top on it just like the Chicago Tribune Building. So I just said, 'Ray, cut the top off, just cut it off.'"

And so, according to Frank Lloyd Wright, that is how the top of the *Daily News* Building came to be the way it is. It was characteristic at any rate for Raymond Hood that he shared his interest in what he was doing with visitors from in town and out of town.

Unlike other architects who have been satisfied to square off the tops of their buildings as uncompromisingly as possible, in this case at least Hood was not. If you look carefully at the top, the Daily News has an entasis like a Greek column. An entasis is "a slight convex curvature from the vertical outline of the shaft of a pilaster or column," according to the dictionary, and not only do the pilasters or piers of the *Daily News* curve inward, but so do all the spandrel recesses in between. There are some seventy five in all, and every one is different.

The *Daily News* Building, like its predecessor the American Radiator Building, was cited by the New York Landmarks Commission. In the book, *New York Landmarks,* the citation reads:

> "Daily News Building, 220 East 42nd Street. Acclaimed for its verticality, this building was considered by many as the embodiment of the soaring quality of the skyscraper. However, the vertical ribbons of equal width fail to express the location of the steel columns; and, as seen from within, the fenestration—a series of solids and voids—represents no improvement over that of the eighteenth century.

From what I have written, it is clear that I am at variance with the opinions in this tribute to the *Daily News.* From the viewpoint of twenty-five years, I think the *Daily News* Building not only was, but remains one of the highest achievements in expressing the soaring quality of the skyscraper.

"Vertical ribbons of equal widths" need not express the location of the steel columns, and to me this exemplifies the difference between an abstract theory of architecture and the logic of someone like Raymond Hood.

The facts seem quite contrary to the criticism: "as seen from within the fenestration—a series of solids and voids—represents no improvement over the eighteenth century," for as far as office buildings go, the fenestration of the *Daily News* represents a culmination of the idiom of separate windows.

A totally new era and a totally new approach were to come after the Depression, and there was good reason for the whole technique of office building design to change. With the coming of air conditioning, ventilation was no longer to depend on windows, in fact they were to be fastened shut; having them opened by individuals would "unbalance the system" as well as let in the dirt from outside, dirt which air conditioning would filter out.

There was no longer the same degree of dependence on natural light, now that there were entire ceilings of fluorescent light. This made interim spaces away from the windows as valuable as those near the windows for working purposes, because of artificial light and ventilation. The necessity foreseen by Raymond Hood, of getting rid of intervening structural columns became more obvious with this deeper space.

The added expense of heavier steel girders and fewer columns was now justified by the special requirements of the complete air conditioning. Now extensive ducts in the ceilings were required to distribute the air, and deeper beams so that this space between them could provide space for housing the ducts above the ceilings. This made the floor to floor height greater than in the old buildings. On the horizontal floor plan, partitions were less desirable and open type offices came into greater use, for the better and more economical distribution of artificial light and conditioned air. Greatly improved use of accoustical materials made this method practical. These new conditions were reflected architecturally by continuous strips of windows instead of the previous era's single windows.

New theories and new architects came over from Europe, with the new era, as reflected in the following incident: In the office of Wallace K. Harrison, it was my job at this later time to review the plans of others instead of drawing them myself. One young draftsman, imbued with the new spirit, wanted me to see one of the first buildings in Cambridge by the German emigré Walter Gropius.

Gropius' new building proved to be a small one story kindergarten, and what was remarkable to me was that, despite the fact that the minimum wall of eight inches required by the building code would have no trouble in holding up a one story roof, the space inside was full of seemingly unnecessary lolly columns, round steel pipes filled with concrete.

Daily News Building from east on 41st Street.
courtesy of the author

On my return from Cambridge, I reviewed my trip with the young designer, saying I liked everything about the building, except that I couldn't see why all those columns were out in the work space. If any principle of architecture had been learned from the late Raymond Hood, it should have been to locate the columns in the outside walls or wall of enclosures that had to be there anyway—instead of in everybody's way.

This logic did not convince my young friend, who asserted that today anybody knows "that every effort should be made to locate the columns in the space where they can be seen. In this way they lend a feeling of sense of support."

It sounded to me like a new twist to the "Faith in God story" I heard when I first entered Hood's office. Considering that the fundamental purpose of architecture is to enclose space for the actual use of people, Raymond Hood's logic seems to be more relevant than such theories, however widely followed and respected by the next generation.

Going over to the *Daily News* later to check on the citation, I was happy to find the plaque on the building inscribed as follows:

LANDMARKS OF NEW YORK
NEW YORK DAILY NEWS BUILDING
Completed in 1930 from design of
John Mead Howells and Raymond Hood
this structure was cited in 1957 by the
Municipal Art Society and the
Society of Architectural Historians
"for originality in design and
influence on later work."
Plaque erected 1957 by
New York Community Trust

The Education of an Apprentice

The education of the beginning architect sometimes took on other forms than that of the drafting room. With Hood, one of these was client relationships. One time I came to his office as a gentleman was leaving, apparently an old friend. Once out of hearing, Mr. Hood said, "Only client I ever threw out of the office."

"How was that?" I asked.

"Well, this man was in the drapery business down in the sweatshop district of the thirties. Apparently he had made a success of it and the idea came to him that he could do better yet. At that time the 'smart shop' district had moved up into the forties, near Fifth Avenue. In the American Radiator Building which was just completed, there was a fine high-ceilinged show room space available on the ground floor. He rented the space and came in to see me about fixing it up."

"Now Mr. Hood, as I say, the time has come to move up into the smart neighborhood and I want to do things right—in style, quality, everything in character with my success in business."

"What do you mean by right?" Hood quoted himself as having said.

"Doing it in marble—to the ceiling. Expense is no concern," the prospective client had said. Nonetheless, he hesitated, "perhaps I should know about how much it would cost."

Hood did a little figuring and gave him an estimate.

The client swallowed, and then said "Mr. Hood, as you say, it is an awfully high ceiling. While expense is no item, still, thinking of the character of my business, don't you think marble to the ceiling might be a little ostentatious? Perhaps it might rub people the wrong way. Might not something a little quieter have a little more class?"

Hood said that was true and that finishing the job in travertine would really be a better thing to do.

"As I said, expense is not a consideration, but what would travertine cost?"

Hood did some more calculating and quoted a lower price. The client hesitated again: perhaps even travertine sounded as though he was trying to show off a bit; maybe wood would be a better solution, say walnut paneling, more dignified and conservative, with more class. . . . Mr. Hood refigured and again cost was substantially lower.

Still the man hesitated, "When you think of it, even walnut to the ceiling would seem extravagant to some people. How would it look if the walnut were to go up three-quarters or even halfway, with a quiet painted plaster wall above, or decorated with stenciling?"

Hood said this, too could be designed to look all right and would cost still less money. "However, I have a suggestion to make . . ." Hood explained his proposed plan for the client to follow step by step:

"You say you want to move uptown into a high class neighborhood and do something in style and in character with your business. All right, I'll tell you: Just go out and hire a carpenter and tell him you want to put a dado, no, not even a dado, just a walnut base six inches high around the room.

"You will have quality, be in character with your business, and save a lot of money." After a pause, Hood added, "You know who you remind me of? A man who buys a box at the opera and then goes in his overalls!"

The client stalked out of the room.

In a few days he was back. "Mr. Hood, I've been thinking over what you said. We're going to do the job and do it right, in marble, to the ceiling."

For me, attending the meetings on the *Daily News* Building was as often as not another kind of lesson in human relations. When we had plans complete enough for an estimate of cost and operation they were sent out in advance to all concerned. About two weeks later a meeting was called to coordinate the findings.

Hood sat at the head of the table. The major point under consideration was the cost of construction. The first question was addressed to the contractor: "Mr. Hegeman," said Hood, "now that you have figured out the cost in some detail, for comparative purposes, what does the figure come to per cubic foot?"

It was something like a dollar and twenty cents, as I remember vaguely, almost twice as much as the typical office building going up in New York then, and nearly as much as the elaborate new Grand Central Building astride Park Avenue with its pyramidal roof in gold leaf.

"How can this be?" exclaimed Hood, obviously upset. "We've designed the simplest, most efficient building we can and you come up with a price like that?"

Hegeman hedged his quotation around with a lot of impressive reasons that sounded big but were only small shrubbery. Underneath, he too was thinking of the picture on the wall, the *Chicago Tribune* building, which was not only designed by Hood, but which he himself had built.

Architects always talked little plans, he knew, at the start and ended up big. He wasn't going to be fooled. "Besides, young man," he told me after the meeting, "there's one thing I've learned over these many years, and don't you ever forget it—it's the first price that sticks in the client's mind."

When the real estate people, who were also playing safe, were questioned, it developed it would cost more to operate and maintain the building than the rents could bring in, let alone any question of profit on the operation. It was clear the project was in the red before it was out of the ground. Hood then announced, "Gentlemen, do you know what you have just succeeded in doing? You have figured yourselves out of a job."

Everyone rushed back to his office to sharpen his pencil, and we got busy too. Noontimes found me scurrying around finding out what rents the buildings in the Grand Central zone were getting, what they cost to operate, and how much they cost to build.

When the next building meeting came around, Hood carefully refrained from asking the "experts" their opinion on anything. Instead, he asked them questions to which we already had the answers. All he wanted was confirmation by the "expert." Instead of asking Mr. Hegeman how much the building would cost, he asked the costs of buildings on all sides of it. If, according to Mr. Hegeman the Chrysler Building was seventy-two cents, the Fred F. French Building sixty-five cents, and the Chanin Building sixty-nine cents, then Hood deduced, it was reasonable the *Daily News* Building might cost sixty-eight cents or seventy cents.

Similarly, the rentals and the cost of maintenance of comparable buildings were boxed in. The "experts" were firmly led by Hood to come up with reasonable figures to use for the budget, substantiated by practice in the neighborhood. Once more the project was back on the track.

Various Projects

Once Hood was released from the Gothic idiom, it was characteristic of him not to strive to develop a style of his own, but to try a new approach with each project. Soon after the *Daily News* Building, Hood entered into a commercial venture with Kenneth Murchison, a fellow architect. It was to be the Beaux Arts Apartments, and the two architects contributed the plans as their part of the investment.

The name came from the Beaux Arts Building, just completed as a headquarters by the Society of Beaux Arts Architects, a few doors up the street from the apartment house site. The latest idea on a convenient home in the city was a one room apartment with a strip kitchen in the back wall, and a bath. Two lots were assembled on opposite sides of 44th Street so they would complete a small bit of the urban picture.

The standardized apartments repeated each other on the different floors, either side of a central corridor. In step with the latest feeling in "modern" design the exterior was expressed in horizontal bands of white brick at each floor, quite a contrast to the vertical lines of the *Daily News* two blocks away. The front wall of each living room was filled with casement windows from wall to wall, and the piers between the apartments were in red and black brick. This created an alternating dark band with the white.

The center portion of each facade was set back a few feet from the street line, except those of the apartments at either end. This gave the end apartments a chance to have a corner window. Subject to being convinced by the young in the office that it would greatly improve the daylighting of the end apartments, Hood for the first time left out any expression of a corner pier or column. He was indeed in step with the design innovations of the times.

In the early thirties, Hood greatly admired a rather independent and enterprising distributor of G.E. refrigerators, Rex Cole, for his energy and imagination. At the time, the characteristic symbol of the product was the circular compressor on the top. A mock-up of this device, if not the whole refrigerator, was used on the top of the two or three showrooms Hood designed for Cole. The building at Bay Ridge and the one in Flushing were both equally up to date in their design, distinguished by their use of color: in one case shades of gray painted on steel plates with vermilion stripes, and the other white brick with red tile bands.

Rex Cole showroom.
courtesy of McGraw-Hill

Beaux Arts Apartments, New York, by Raymond Hood and Kenneth Murchison.
courtesy of the author

Capt. Patterson's House, Ossining, N.Y.   ·   *courtesy of McGraw-Hill*

Capt. Patterson was, as always, the good client; Hood designed an apartment house at 3 East 84th Street for him in 1928. It contained a city residence for the owner. Two years later, Capt. Patterson asked Hood to design a home for his country place in Ossining, N.Y. A somewhat cubistic affair, it was originally intended to be below ground. With today's wide use of air conditioning and fluorescent light, it might be a good idea, but it was not so practical then. And so the house was built above ground, but Capt. Patterson insisted it be camouflaged after the manner of World War I theories. The outlines were presumably to be broken up by irregular patterns of contrasting colors; it was understood that this was not so much to conceal the house as to lose the design.

Capt. Patterson felt that architects, Raymond Hood in particular, tend to locate windows in a house where they look well in the exterior design. The Captain wanted windows located where he wanted them, no matter how they looked. If then, the architect felt he had spoiled his design, then the least the owner could do was paint them out so nobody would notice them. Capt. Patterson's house exhibited many of his idiosyncracies, at least one of which might have had wider application by tired businessmen. In his bathroom Capt. Patterson had a full length mirror installed in front of the toilet; he said that the only time of day he looked relaxed and content was when he was enthroned. It was this expression on his face he did not want to miss.

Scheme for Myrtle Beach Club, South Carolina. Aquatint by Donald Douglas.
courtesy of the author

Interior of steamship for United States
Lines   *courtesy of McGraw-Hill*

The Chicago World's Fair

There were often projects going on in Hood's office that were of a speculative nature for the client, calling for imaginative schemes and presentations. One was the Myrtle Beach Club in South Carolina, for which an elaborate prospectus was made. Illustrations for such work were often aquatints by Donald Douglas, a designer in the office. He had graduated from the Yale Architectural School and had great artistic ability. Raymond greatly admired his work and used it whenever he could. It was a great tragedy that all his plates were destroyed in a fire—they would have been a valuable record in themselves.

Besides the work on the *Daily News,* the office began work on several other large projects, generally in association with other architects. One of these, in collaboration with John Holabird and Ralph Walker, was a project for a great commercial development above the tracks of the Illinois Central freight yards in Chicago, much as had been done in the Grand Central zone in New York.

Another project was for the interiors of a leviathan steamship for the United States Lines, to be a sister ship to the *Manhattan* and the *Constitution.* Neither of these two projects survived the Crash, but one that did was the Chicago World's Fair of 1933.

On Hood's recommendation the Board of Directors of the Fair appointed eight architects to the Board of Design. One member was Hood himself, and two others from New York were Harvey Wiley Corbett, who became chairman, and Ralph Walker. Walker said, "The group entered into a series of competitions with each other, and which were without too much basic understanding of exposition buildings."

This may account for the origin of a story by Raymond Hood. Charles Dawes, a director of the Fair, became impatient and decided to bring in a consultant who had some knowledge of what Fairs were all about. He invited Sir John Cole, architect of the Wembley Exposition, to come over from England and meet the architects of the Fair. After reviewing the various schemes, Sir John decided they were much too elaborate and far fetched.

"Actually," he said, "the design of a Fair is very simple. The object is to lead the largest number of people by the greatest linear footage of exhibits with the least amount of building. All you have to do is work out some unit form of pavilion in which the people come in one end, weave by the exhibits, and go out the other in the most efficient way. Then you obtain the estimates of the area of exhibition space required. Dividing by the square feet per pavilion, gives you the number of pavilions required.

Scheme for Chicago World's Fair, 1933, by Raymond Hood   *courtesy of McGraw-Hill*

String these together as the site permits, spaced by the size of the crowds expected, and you have the layout for a World's Fair."

Devoid as it was of any recognition of the part imagination should play in a Fair, nobody could deny the logic of this solution. Since there were no questions, and Mr. Dawes looked pleased, it began to look as though the scheme for the Fair was out of American hands.

In the nick of time, Hood spoke up, "John, I mean Sir John, we are very grateful to you for taking the time to come over here and give us the benefit of your experience with great expositions, and we are grateful to Mr. Dawes for making it possible for you to do so. Now that you have given us the idea of what a Fair should be, we can settle down and do the job as it ought to be done, with no more fooling around. However, before we do, Sir John, I would like to ask one question.

"This Wembley Exposition you tell us about, how did it work out? Was it a success? In fact, didn't it fail? For that matter, wasn't it a complete flop?"

That did it, and the architects had one more chance to get back to work. In the end, according to Walker, it was Hood who came up with an idea acceptable to all. Unusual in that it was an asymmetrical scheme, it was a departure in itself from the classic pattern of World's Fairs. The idea came to Hood while on vacation in Amalfi. Hurrying back to Paris he collected together all of his "boys" he could find, which included Louis Skidmore, Carl Landerfelt, and Frank Roorda. In the manner of the old student "charette" they batted out the scheme in ten days and got it off on the boat to Chicago.

While Hood succeeded in bringing all the architects together on one scheme, the final design was developed in eight sections, which were assigned to the individual architects by lot. Each architect was responsible for coordination with his neighbor for sections on either side of his assignment. In this way, the architects felt they avoided "committee architecture," expressed their individuality and achieved variety. Although I did not work on Hood's scheme, it was nearby in the drafting room. Characteristically, Hood delighted in showing it off to whoever came in the office. One day he brought out a prepossessed young man disguised by heavy dark sunglasses.

Raymond Hood's model for G.E. Building Interior, Chicago's World's Fair, 1933.
courtesy of the author

The man sat down in front of the drawing and listened attentively while Hood explained it all. At the end, Hood said, "Well, how do you like it?"

"Listen, Ray," replied the stranger, "you ought to let me sit down here and work this thing out for you."

As soon as the stranger was out of the room, I went over to my neighbor and said indignantly, "Who does that guy think he is, anyway?"

"That," I was told, "is Norman Bel Geddes."

This is another story that shows Hood's typical pleasure in sharing his interest in what he was doing with the visitor who came into his office. He wasn't "selling" himself or his ideas so much as revealing an interest in what others might think, and he appreciated the lay opinion as much as that of the expert. He made his visitor feel a part of what was going on.

Norman Bel Geddes' point of view brings to mind Frank Lloyd Wright, whose great master, Louis Sullivan, had also been an individualist. This hadn't prevented the chosen group of Architects of the Chicago Fair of 1893 from seeing that Sullivan had a chance to do a building of his own. Now there was another Fair and another outstanding figure on the sidelines.

I once asked Hood why Frank Lloyd Wright was not included. He said they all wanted him but when the subject was broached, Wright had said he would be glad to work on the Fair provided the architects resigned and left the entire job up to him. It is what you would have expected him to say.

Some time after the development of the preliminary sketches for the Fair there was a meeting at the Town Hall in New York which Donald Douglas and I attended. Both Frank Lloyd Wright and Hood were on the platform as guests, and I have long since forgotten what the meeting was all about, but I have retained a feeling it was the beginning of a conscious effort to turn the spotlight on the long obscured Frank Lloyd Wright and help give him the place and opportunity he deserved in American architecture.

Like many a lesser light in those days, Wright was having a difficult time, and Hood, as President of the Architectural League, had been instrumental in getting together some money to help him out. One thing I remember clearly, however, is that Donald Douglas and I came away so mad we could spit, because of the way Raymond Hood had been treated on this occasion. My inquiries as to what actually took place at the meeting had about reached a dead end when Douglas Haskell, retired editor of the *Architectural Forum* told me I would find an account of it written up by Wright himself in the First Edition of *An Autobiography* published in 1932. The story from which this is taken is called "A Week in New York:"

Although it was a little late, apparently some people in New York had wondered why Frank Lloyd Wright had not been asked to join the other architects of the Chicago Fair, at least to the extent of designing a building. It was believed the "Eastern Architects," presumably Hood and Corbett, "with the power of selecting their Chicago confrères, had omitted him (without so much as a consultation) for fear he would 'seek to dominate' and might not cooperate. . . ."

There were two or three meetings in New York which Mr. Wright did attend, although he felt the issue of whether or not he would participate in the Fair was something of a post mortem and that the agenda hardly represented his own feelings in the matter.

According to Wright's story, the night before the Town Hall meeting, he had been the guest of the Women's University Club in Brooklyn: the subject was Modern Architecture and both Hood and Corbett were there as guests. Concerning the Fair and the fact that Wright was not one of the architects, Corbett had said, "But Frank Lloyd Wright will not stay in line. Frank Wright never does stay in line."

By the time Wright's turn came to speak the affair had dragged on too long in a warm evening. He would have dropped the matter, but the audience insisted he reply. Wright said he noted that, "only eclectics who had put the masks on the skyscrapers of New York were invited. . . ." referring to Hood and Corbett, "the Fair is the latest expression of the New York eclectic modernism," the architects "crowding to be the first to be modern."

Wright realized he had said too much for a polite meeting, but continued:

> "I said what I thought and felt about the whole hypocritical mess being made by the eclectics arriving at modernism by the adventitious road; sincerely described the Fair as I saw that commercial degenerate performance, the opportune New York Functioneers, 'Wolken Krabbers' climbers onto the latest bandwagon, regardless, determined to hold or drive."

It must, indeed, have been a warm evening. The next night came the meeting at the Town Hall, apparently arranged a little off the cuff, and like the one the night before, destined to get a little out of hand. Confirming my understanding that he had been invited to join in the Fair, in principle at least, was the following statement of Wright:

> "Already I had given plenty of good reasons for such non-employment and was ready to give more. It was surely better to have one architect out of employment in these parlous times than the eight or ten already employed in the Fair. Another group entirely would have come with me."

111

The hall was packed; the speakers were at their best—Alexander Woollcott "efflorescent."

"At least," said Wright, "living in New York does keen the rapier and polish the thrust. . . . Gaiety changed when Mumford began to speak." It was Hood, the invited guest, who had to sit there and take this: no wonder those of us from his office were so mad we could spit, not at Frank Lloyd Wright, but the speakers of the evening, whose "rapiers" were not only sharpened and polished, but long enough to reach the back seats. What Wright went on to say seems very pertinent in a way to this story; after lambasting the architects and architecture of the Fair he notes,

> "It would seem I spoke because I 'resented' being left out by the Commission whereas I resent only their quick turnover and pretentious scene painting as unworthy of modern architecture."

Wright went on to give three ideas of what he thought the Fair could have been:

> "Instead of the old stage props of the previous fair, miles of picture buildings faked in cheap materials wrapped around a lagoon, fountain or theatrical waterfall, let there be a genuine construction, something worthy of the Century of Progress."

"The Fair itself, the Apotheosis of the skyscraper!" Wright had the idea of a tremendous skyscraper 250 stories high with the Fair spread on the various floors, left open so even the clouds, artificial if necessary, could sift in.

Wright's second idea was "Steel in Tension" (Roebling—"the structures of the Fair suspended on cables from great pylons.") The third was "Chicago Harbor:" the foundation of the whole fair on pontoons subject to the motion of the water in the lagoon.

All of these were imaginative ideas, but much too late. Don Douglas and I felt the literary people were victimizing Raymond Hood to make a show for their revered hero, Frank Lloyd Wright. Hood had never reached such philosophic levels. He had been given the theme of the Fair, "A Century of Progress," and sought only a plan that would successfully handle the crowds and enter the spirit of a great exhibition.

CHAPTER **V**

RAYMOND HOOD,
JOHN R. TODD
AND RADIO CITY

Metropolitan Square

On account of illness, I had to stay away from the office for a short time in the fall of 1929. Rather late in the day of my return Mr. Hood came around to my board to see how I was. Sympathetically, he said, "This working all day and night doesn't pay. You'd better cut it out from now on."

After a pause, he added, "By the way, I have a scheme here for a three block development in New York. You don't think you could have something worked out by morning, do you?"

I did, and that was my introduction to the future Radio City. At that time the project was known as Metropolitan Square and it called for a business development of three city blocks 920 feet long and each 200 feet wide, on the site of the future Rockefeller Center. From a business point of view, the costs of the land rental, mortgages and taxes in this zone would require almost a maximum development of the available area for business purposes. I understood the project had started as a center for a new Opera House, but it had been found economically impossible and the idea had been dropped.

The enterprise was under the direction of John R. Todd, a well known contractor and speculative builder and friend of John D. Rockefeller, Jr.

John R. Todd, building manager of Rockefeller Center. *Courtesy of* American Magazine

He had his own architects, a comparatively young firm named Reinhard and Hofmeister. To lend experience and prestige to this enterprise, perhaps, Harvey Corbett and Raymond Hood had been called in as consultants. The group worked independently at the start and our plans were titled Raymond Hood, Architect, rather than the firm name.

Hood was excited by the prospects. I recall that shortly after, he took me to a joint meeting in the Graybar Building, and on the way over in a taxi started to tell me that he thought the great day for architects had really come. Here he was working on the design for a new steamship for the United States Lines, the Chicago World's Fair, and a project for covering over the tracks of the Illinois Central Railroad in Chicago, a much greater development than the Grand Central Zone. Now came the project for a three block development in the heart of New York.

I was not quite so elated. I said it didn't seem to me that this was on his way up as an architect, but a step down. It was a great project, but this time he wasn't an architect dealing directly with his client, but was reduced to dealing through his agent, in this case, John R. Todd, and that might not be so easy, from what I had heard. That was enough to spoil that conversation, and the rest of the trip was in silence.

While the architects worked in their offices the first few months, they held joint meetings in the Graybar Building with Todd to review their various ideas. Shortly after, the three architects were organized into one firm with a mouthful of a name: Reinhard and Hofmeister, Corbett, Harrison and MacMurray, Raymond Hood, Godley and Fouilhoux. Putting that footage on every plan gave the draftsman writer's cramp. A new joint drafting room was set up in the Graybar Building with a few representatives from each office at first, six or eight all told. Part of a joint organization working in a common office, I was no longer working directly with Mr. Hood, but continued to be at some of the architects' meetings when he came over.

About the actual contract with the architects, I heard from Francis Christie, the lawyer for Rockefeller Center, of his showing the document to Hood to look over. Raymond perused it carefully and then remarked that it contained twenty-nine pages of how to fire the architect and only one on the architect's rights.

The Graybar Standard

Todd, Robertson and Todd, the managers of the Rockefeller Center project, were well known builders in New York. They had put up fine structures such as the Cunard Building near the Battery. They were also speculative builders; as for their investment, they had put up buildings such as the Graybar Building, where the three firms of architects established their combined office. The Graybar Building, situated at the Lexington Avenue entrance to the Grand Central Terminal as well as the subway and shuttle, was a great success due to its strategic location. Its success did not prevent it from becoming a great experiment in waterproofing a building after it was finished. The walls were sliced a little thin, and they leaked.

Under the particular circumstances of ownership and financial success, if there was one single criterion for the future Rockefeller Center, it was still "the Graybar standard." But if there was anything the architects hoped, it was that Rockefeller Center would not be just another "Graybar Building." The problem wasn't one of bettering a specification of materials and methods, it was one of overcoming a state of mind: that if the Graybar Building was a financial success then everything else about it must be perfect.

As the overall scheme began to crystallize, various studies and schemes were tried for the layout of the tower buildings of which the central core of stairs, elevators and toilets was the critical element. This core may take up a small percentage of any one floor but it takes spaces out of all floors from top to bottom. As I was working on these schemes one day, Mr. Todd came by. Given the size of the elevator cabs, I had worked hard to figure out the minimum enclosing structure. Todd asked how big the cabs were. I replied that they were the same as the Graybar Building. Then he asked about the total length over a bank of four elevators. About four feet less than those in the Graybar Building was the answer.

Todd said, "Make it the same as the Graybar." Nobody in his right mind tried to argue with John R. Todd, but I tried to explain that the spacing in the Graybar was not determined by the minimum structural requirements, but by the spacing of the railroad tracks in the terminal down below. Todd shut me up with, "The Graybar has the best elevator service in the city—not two minutes wait between cars. Make it the same." He went off, and I took my watch and went out in the lobby to time the interval between cars.

When Mr. Hood came by, I told him of my experience, how I found a way to save four feet of space all the way through the building only to be told to throw it away. And as for Todd's two-minute elevators, I had timed the elevators: the service was most irregular, with nothing like two minutes between cars.

"You know what the trouble is, of course," replied Hood, "You can't tell Mr. Todd anything because he knows. You see, he owns the building. Whenever he is in his office on the top floor they keep a cab waiting. Whenever he is out of the building they keep a cab waiting on the ground floor. He never has to wait, not even two minutes. He thinks the system is perfect."

Prometheus Unveiled

In the plans there was a small plaza at the foot of the great central skyscraper. Where an esplanade led to it from Fifth Avenue between two low buildings there was an opportunity to create a restful feature. Hood wanted a fountain. At the next meeting he presented the idea: they were piling up great masses of prosaic office space, dwarfing the streets, and concentrating great hordes of people to spill out on them at the hours of change.

Having piled up these storied walls, baking in the sun, stifling the streets below, said Hood, perhaps they should give back a little something to the man in the street. On a good hot summer day on the crowded sidewalks, what would it take to have the sound of a little cool running water, perhaps even a fountain splashing in the plaza at the foot of the tower . . . a world of difference.

Dedicated, practical, hard-headed men ran this business enterprise: "A fountain?" They came down on Mr. Hood like a ton of bricks, true to form. Almost sputtering, John R.'s brother, Dr. Todd asked Hood if he had any idea what it would mean to have a fountain, with running water at that.

"Why, do you realize this would mean recirculating 30,000 gallons of water a day?"

"And how much," obliged Hood in a tired voice, "would it cost to recirculate 30,000 gallons of water a day?"

Todd scratched and figured away for a moment or two and finally came up with the answer: "To recirculate 30,000 gallons of water," he said, "would cost $8.30 a day." Even to a hard headed business man in an enterprise then estimated at $250,000,000, $8.30 a day didn't seem such an appalling extravagance after all. The fountain went in, and became the famous Prometheus Fountain of the sculptor Paul Manship.

Are You Sure?

With all the schemes being tried out in the office by any number of planners, and none of them seeming to reach a satisfactory conclusion, it was not long before John R. Todd began to get impatient. The basic problem had no ready-made solution; no matter how good a scheme might be from the architectural point of view, weighing all the factors that go into a satisfactory piece of design, the overriding consideration was of economic feasibility.

What this meant in plain figures was earning ten million dollars after overhead. A third of this sum, roughly speaking, was needed to pay the ground rent to Columbia University, another third to the City in taxes, and finally the balance to pay the interest on the mortgage of the Metropolitan Life Insurance Co., which was providing the building money. The overall cost of the enterprise was then estimated at some $250,000,000.

This implied a lot of rentable space and the question of the best way to stack it up. Every adequate scheme for the amount of space provided had to be evaluated for potential income and compared with previous schemes. Since to stack up the floors till the required square footage was acquired would hardly be an architectural solution, innumerable plans were piling up, some of them meeting the economic situation.

John Todd was getting more impatient. Finally the day came when he'd had enough. The architects had fooled around a long time looking for a better solution when there was at least one plan that added up. He decided it was time for a decision, made his choice and told the assembled architects that this was it, and to get busy on the working drawings, because it cost a lot of money just to stand still on a project of this size.

The square footage added up all right, but as an overall architectural solution it wasn't very good. None of the architects spoke up, not even Hood, and I didn't see how he could keep still. I knew he felt that any project, big or small, should have at least one good idea behind it to make it worthwhile.

Hood waited until the others had left the room; I hardly counted. "Well, John," he said, "it's certainly a relief to get this thing settled. As you say, we've been fooling around long enough and it's time to get down to work."

"Now that you've decided on a plan we can buckle down and get on with the job. This is good. But one thing, John, in selecting this particular scheme to go ahead with, as something you'd want to build, all things considered, are you sure you're right?"

Todd wasn't sure, and the scheme collapsed. We all got back to work once more. And we realized how little time there was to find a better answer.

The Pickle Business

While Hood was thinking of a structure faced with stone, the Todds, with economy ever in mind as far as architectural efforts were concerned, thought of it as brick. Many extremely interesting studies were made based on the use of brick, of treating the elevation of the skyscraper in contrasting patterns. But it was obvious that the eventual design would be just plain brick, to save money.

From Hood's point of view, something had to be done. He waited until he had Todd alone. "John, you know, I was thinking over what you said about building Radio City of brick, and come to think of it, it might not be such a bad idea," began Hood diplomatically. "After all, this is just

119

(*Opposite page*) The Prometheus Fountain, Lower Plaza, Rockefeller Center.

courtesy of Rockefeller Center

another commercial building and its purpose is to make money. The cheaper you can build it, and still keep the rain out, the better chance you have to come out ahead.

"After all, a building in its appearance, should express the kind of an enterprise it is. If the purpose is to make as much money as it can at the least investment cost, then brick is good enough, even common brick. In fact, when you come right down to it, if corrugated iron—painted, of course, is good enough for the purpose then that is what should be used."

Todd took out his ear plugs. "Corrugated iron, did you say?"

Hood seemed to hedge a little. "Well, not exactly, but seriously, John, a few years ago we did a building in Chicago for an important company, a newspaper business. Although they didn't feel they themselves had anything to express worth spending money on, they did realize they were putting up something on the Chicago skyline for all the people to see.

"They decided, whatever they put up, they wanted the people of Chicago to be proud of what they did. You know, they spent a million dollars extra, to make the exterior of that building in carved limestone—but, my God, if I were in the pickle business!"

From that day on the material of Radio City was to be limestone.

Roof Gardens

If the Todds, John R. and "Doctor" Todd, seemed a little hard-boiled when it came to spending money on those little things that make all the difference, it must be remembered that they had the drive, the foresight and courage to persevere with this great enterprise at a time when everything else was falling apart. If they were to bring all this space on the market at a time when space could be had for the asking, they had to have as low a rent as possible for something better than anyone else. To spend money to landscape the roofs of Radio City seemed about as far fetched an idea as anyone would ever dream of presenting to the Todds. Raymond Hood bided his time.

One day John R. Todd was standing in the conference room, about twenty-six floors up in the Graybar Building, looking out the window. Hood came over and began looking out, too. "Mess, isn't it?" he said. "Look at all those roofs down there cluttered up with bulkheads, ventilators, chimneys, elevator penthouses, water tanks, and God knows what else."

He paused a moment to let the scene register and then said, "By the way, John, thinking of Radio City and getting the best possible rents for the space, I was wondering if office space that looked out on a garden would be worth any more than, say space that just looked out on another roof?"

120

First model for roof gardens.
courtesy of the author

Roof garden on the RCA
Building.
courtesy of Wendall MacRae

"What do you mean, gardens, in a place like New York?"

"Well, compared to looking out over a mess like this, suppose it looked out over something like Bryant Park, wouldn't that kind of space be worth more per square foot?"

At that time Robert Moses had just done an excellent job redesigning and planting Bryant Park.

Todd allowed it would indeed be worth more, perhaps a dollar a square foot more.

"A dollar, you say . . ." Hood appeared to be searching for something he couldn't quite find. "A dollar . . . Mr. Todd!" he said with a note of excitement in his voice, "do you know there will be about seven acres of roof over the lower parts of Radio City? A lot of office space will look out over those roofs. At a dollar more per square foot extra you could afford to landscape those roofs like the hanging gardens of Babylon."

Not long afterward, the architectural sculptor, René Chambellan was indicating foliage in plasticine on the model of the roofs, and I was working out a system of wire netting that would retain the roots of trees so they wouldn't blow over in the relatively shallow soil when the winds blew.

The Todds went even further. When the time came, they didn't spend money landscaping the roof, they leased out this privilege of doing so as a "concession" to a landscape nursery to use as a showroom. Under Ralph Hancock, the noted landscape gardener, three acres of beautiful garden were developed, and the idea itself spread down to the street. Today one of the favorite sights at Eastertime is the wonderful display of flowers and plants leading down through the promenade from Fifth Avenue to the fountain of Prometheus. The gardens are still there, and again, at Eastertime, some of the roofs bordering the plaza are further embellished with potted flowers and plants.

The Coffee Pot

As the plans developed, it was my privilege to have all sorts of other things to do besides drafting plans; one was investigating the methods and materials that might be used for the buildings. Hundreds of samples of stone, brick and beautiful marble were collected; some of the latter were two by four feet. Like the ancient Romans, we could choose from Numidian Brèche Sanguine from Morocco to Cipolin green from the islands of Greece.

I was often the one to interview the salesmen who came in with something of special interest; the office itself was under a state of siege in those days of thin pickings, from those who had something to sell. No matter what, they tried.

One day I was asked to see a very distinguished Southern gentleman with irresistible door-opening references. Apparently he had just disembarked from the train from Georgia and our office was his first stop. He owned a mountain of stone just outside Atlanta, as proof of which he brought along snapshots showing rocky ledges through the trees.

"Mr. Kilham," he began, "down there in Georgia a friend of mine heard about your building a skyscraper, and he said that to do it you're going to need a lot of stone. So I got right on the train and came up here. They say the man to see is you. Mr. Kilham, I have enough stone in that mountain to build the whole thing."

I was as polite as the occasion called for and duly impressed. Still, owning a mountain doesn't mean it is suitable for building, nor does it open a quarry, much less cut the stone and transport it to New York. However, I assured him we would keep it in mind, if not our files, together with the snapshots of the mountain. He prepared to leave.

"By the way, Mr. Kilham, besides the mountain, I also have an elephant to sell, if there is some way you could find use for that too."

Not long after this a young man arrived with an introduction to Mr. Hood. He insisted on seeing him. Mr. Hood was busy and asked if I would find out what it was all about and stand him off if I could. The young man represented a firm that had "a service to render to architects." They had learned from the newspapers that Radio City was getting under way and would include office buildings, shops, stores and theatres, etc.

The young man had come over as fast as he could. "Mr. Kilham, we want to help you out. We're prepared to design anything, we don't care whether it's a theatre or a doorway or an office building or a ventilator—whatever it is, we are ready. We can do it in our own shop, or, if you prefer, we can send men over here to do it right on your own boards."

"This is indeed an unusual service to render to architects. Tell me, have you ever done anything of this nature before?"

"Most certainly," answered the young man confidently. "In fact, I think I have something here that will interest you intensely." He searched in his brief case and came up with an eight by ten glossy photograph.

Not quite prepared for what it seemed to represent, I thought I had better ask. "And just what is it?"

"This," he said, "is a coffee pot we are designing for the Aluminum Company of America."

Since he insisted, I went back to Mr. Hood to see if there was the slightest chance he would see him. I gave a brief account of what had transpired. He said no, he was most certainly too busy to see the young man.

"Then what shall I tell him?"

Mr. Hood smiled. "Tell him we've got the job already."

Art and the Businessman

If the project was a tough economic problem it was also in the hands of a hard-boiled, capable management. It was surprising, therefore, that the idea of creating opportunities for artists to contribute to the enterprise received any consideration at all. That's not to say the Todds were unsympathetic. When the idea of murals was first discussed, Dr. Todd said he had no objections at all, "as long as they are cheaper than plaster." I believe he was under the impression murals were painted on celotex and he would be able to save even more money because the paint job would somehow be free.

The entrance lobby is the place where all the tenants must stand and wait, and the owner generally strives to make his best impression at this point; the ground floor elevator doors in a commercial building set the character of the building, like the doors by Ghiberti for the Baptistry in Florence. One day, while an architects' meeting reviewing designs for these doors was in progress, young Webster Todd of Todd and Brown, the management firm dealing with the contractors, happened to look into the room.

Observing what we were doing Webster Todd said, "I don't know why all you fellows are wasting so much time designing the elevator doors. Dr. Todd is signing the contract for them with the Dahlstrom Co. this very minute."

Now the Dahlstrom Co. was a large manufacturer of metal doors and trim. An anxious call was put through and Dr. Todd said he would be right down. Mr. Reinhard explained to him that the design for the doors wasn't finished; how could he be signing the contract? The lobby doors were not to be just the standard ones used throughout the building, but something distinctive for the entrance of an important building.

Dr. Todd was all reassurance. "Calm yourself, there's nothing to worry about. You can have any design for the door you like, of any fine material you like, as long, that is, as it comes out of the Dahlstrom Catalog."

In the end, somehow or other, the desired doors were obtained, and as time went on John R. Todd began to get into the spirit of things. The architects found there were many places on the buildings where paintings and sculpture could be used to good effect. It was decided, therefore, to hold an evening meeting to bring together a number of artists who would be considered for jobs. There the general conditions under which their work would be done would be explained. John Todd addressed the meeting, saying he was pleased they would be participants in the project and he looked forward to having their creations an integral part of the structures.

However, if he understood things correctly, an artist was a temperamental soul and nobody was going to push him around. For example, you didn't tell him when a piece of sculpture had to be finished, you just waited around until he had an idea and felt like executing it. Whenever it got on the job was time enough.

Todd said that kind of attitude would receive little sympathy, and that at the start the managers had been severely criticized because they were not going to give artists a chance. If it was true artists weren't being given the chance they once had in times past, it was for the simple reason that they did not seem to realize the way things had to be done today. If they wanted to share in the design of modern commercial buildings, then they could expect to work under the same conditions as any other designer, such as the architects and the engineers.

Todd cited the first criterion of a commercial enterprise as "time is money." Then time lost would be money lost, and if the project was to be done on time, every part of it had to be done on the same schedule. Before the steel could be manufactured, the design for it had to be completed. Before the stone could be cut, the architects' layouts had to be complete. Likewise, if one of the sculptors was to have a piece of carving that was to go in place over a door, when the crane lowered the hook to hoist it in place, the carved stone had to be right there. If they were willing to accept such conditions, Todd would welcome the artists as part of the team. If not, the door was open.

Nobody left, and from time to time many others, many of them eminent, were called in as consultants in various capacities. Whether these people were called in for the benefit of their advice, or for the sake of their prominence in their fields, most of them took their work on the project seriously.

Among those consulted was Dr. Hartley Burr Alexander, a professor of the University of Nebraska, who had worked with Goodhue on the Nebraska State Capitol. Now that the opportunities for artists had been determined, it was felt someone should write up the story of Radio City and what it meant. This information, guidance, if not inspiration could be distributed to the individual artists; as a guide to the project it would provide a common thread for the work.

Dr. Alexander worked very hard to prepare the document, and upon completion, brought it to New York to present to John R. Todd. No sooner was the meeting over than he came down to see Hood; he needed sympathy and he needed it badly. Mr. Hood, at least, would understand.

I happened to be in the room at the time Dr. Alexander came in, quite dejected. Hood asked what the trouble was.

"Well, as you know, I have been working very hard on this project which I have called "The Theme Song of Radio City." Today I presented it to Mr. Todd. Instead of showing some sign of appreciation and understanding, he practically threw me out of the office. Why—why—I've never been treated like this before in my life!"

"And you're distressed about this?" asked Hood.

"I certainly am."

"You say you've worked very hard on the theme song. Is it your first try?"

"First try? Why, I've worked hard on this for many weeks—months, even. This is the result of my best effort," affirmed Dr. Alexander.

"And all he did was throw you out of the office, and you're upset and discouraged?"

"Why, yes," said Dr. Alexander, a kindly old gentleman who had obviously never been up against anything quite like this before, "I certainly am."

Then Hood looked at me and asked, "Hey, you, how many schemes did you draw up for Radio City?"

"Thirty-four," I answered.

"How many of them were thrown out?"

"Thirty-four."

Turning to Dr. Alexander, Hood said, "As you can see, we're not downhearted."

The work of many artists eventually found a place in the fabric of the buildings, in stone, canvas, metal and mosaics. The sculptured figure of Prometheus in the Lower Plaza Fountain, for example, and behind it, carved into the three doorways of the RCA Building are the figures of Wisdom, Light and Sound by Lee Lawrie. Against a black background over the entrance to the British Building are a series of gold figures representing industries of the British Empire, by Paul Jennewein. Gaston Lachaise carved panels for a similar location over the French Building.

These, of course, were all well known artists, but with so many people, artists included, out of work, pressure began to arise for giving a chance to some of the unknowns. There would be a place for a large mural in the lobby of the RKO Building, first on the schedule for completion, and a competition was decided upon, both as a chance for some artist and good publicity for Radio City.

The Advisory Committee on Art was invited to select a winner from among the large number of entries received. Among the well known and distinguished committee members were Herbert E. Winlock, director of the Metropolitan Museum of Art, Prof. Everett V. Meeks, Dean of the Yale

School of Fine Arts, Prof. Edward Waldo Forbes, director of the Fogg Museum of Cambridge, together with Prof. Paul J. Sachs of the Fine Arts Department at Harvard and Trustee of the Boston Museum of Fine Arts. Dr. Fiske Kimball, director of the Philadelphia Museum, completed the list.

The pictures were put on display at the University Club; the members of the committee were invited to a dinner which included the architects and Nelson Rockefeller, representing his family interest. The evening grew long with so many pictures and the desire to give each equal and fair consideration. Eventually the choice narrowed down to two paintings, one a good enough picture by a well known artist, recognized by his style; the other, which definitely had the edge, was by an unknown artist whose style was not recognized.

The distinguished jury hemmed and hawed, unable to reach a decision. And a secondary problem had little to do with the quality of the pictures. The jury, men of high reputation were often called upon in their museums to decide whether an obscure painting of a historical period could be attributed to a well known artist. Here, however, they were being asked to stake their reputations on the merits of a work of an artist about whom they could have no assurance whatever.

There was no precedent and they suffered with indecision, while the other guests, anxious to get home, suffered with impatience and fatigue. Finally, to break the deadlock, the youngest of the assemblage, Nelson Rockefeller spoke up: "Gentlemen, we seem to have reached an impasse in the judgment and the time is getting late. If it would help for me to clarify the issue I would sum it up this way: If you select the work of the well known artist and it turns out badly, then it is his fault. If, on the other hand, you choose the work of the unknown artist and it turns out badly, then it is your fault."

This enabled the jury to terminate its deliberations quickly and to reach a conclusion, selecting the work of the well known artist. Still, a lot of new people did have their chance with Radio City.

"I Paint What I See," said Rivera

In the matter of art, however, the Todds were willing to go just so far, and being quick with the right answer didn't mean Raymond Hood always had his way. One day he asked me if I would take a picture for him in the lobby of the skyscraper, or RCA Building, then under construction. Of course I was pleased to do so, but was curious about the reason, "What do you want to prove?"

Hood had been concerned, he said, about the barren effect of the huge, high-ceilinged lobby with nothing in sight but great banks of elevators. That day he had suggested a statue of appropriate size and relevant interest be put there. He had been jumped on like a ton of bricks.

Mr. Brown, of Todd and Brown, had settled the question by stating that it was too late; the building was under construction and the lobby floor already in place, which had not been designed to take the weight of a statue. It couldn't go in there now.

"I would like you to go up there," said Hood to me, "and take a picture in the lobby as it is right now. The ceiling is over thirty feet high. Stored in there until they can use them are piles of building blocks half way up to the ceiling, piles of brick, heaps of sand, bags of lime and cement—tons and tons and tons of stuff. It will hold all that, but it can't stand the weight of a statue. For what comfort it will be I would like to keep the picture on my bureau."

This time Mr. Hood had not found an answer, and his voice was tired. But there was another way of bringing vitality and interest to the great space that had no such limitation, even if a statue was too heavy for the floor of the lobby. The high walls on either side of the banks of elevators, with prime space across the front end opposite the entrance to the building, would be most suitable for some large mural paintings.

This time it was decided to give foreign artists a chance and hold a limited competition; the artists selected for invitation were Matisse, a Frenchman; Picasso, a Spaniard; and Diego Rivera, a Mexican. The reputations of the first two were well established in this country and Rivera's growing. Like Picasso, he had spent many years in Paris, forming many associations, which included Russians.

According to Bertram D. Wolf, from whose life of Rivera comes most of this account, Rivera joined the Communist Party upon returning to Mexico in 1922 after fourteen years abroad. As an artist, he believed his place was not to depict the revolution, but to use his painting as a weapon of revolution. He became a recognized leader, first revealing his great talent and personality in his prodigious murals in fresco for the Ministry of Public Education in Mexico City. As they became known he became world famous, accepted in America as well, despite his dedication to Communism. This acceptance began with his commission by the American Ambassador to Mexico, Dwight P. Morrow, to execute a series of murals on the Conquest in the palace of Cortes at Cuernavaca, and further opportunities came to him in San Francisco and Detroit.

Rivera's introduction to New York came through a meeting at the house of John D. Rockefeller, Jr. on December 9th, 1930, which established the

Mexican Art Association. About the same time, the Museum of Modern Art was set up in the Heckscher Building, exhibiting Rivera's work. Both Mrs. John D. Rockefeller, Jr. and Mrs. Nelson Rockefeller were warm supporters and were instrumental in having him one of those chosen for murals in Rockefeller Center.

Rivera was an outstanding choice as a muralist, with his belief that frescoes should harmonize with the architecture of the building, recognize the use of the building, and have a meaning in the life of the people. With all this it cannot be said his Communist dedication was not recognized as well.

Raymond Hood, who knew French, was chosen as negotiator, and the theme chosen by the Rockefellers for the mural was a mouthful: "Man at the Cross Roads looking with Hope and High Vision to the Choosing of a New and Better Future." An invitation to compete was extended to the three artists, but all three refused. Diego Rivera wrote to Hood that ten years before, as an unknown artist he might have accepted, but today he didn't have to compete with anyone.

Hood telegraphed back that he was sorry. Nelson Rockefeller, however, wouldn't take no for an answer and succeeded in persuading Rivera to accept the commission for the prime location, the wall facing the entrance of the RCA Building, for which he would submit a sketch for approval.

Although he now had the job without having to compete, Rivera objected to being in company with Jose Maria Sert and Frank Brangwyn, who were to do the side walls and for whom Rivera had nothing but contempt. This objection was overcome, and long correspondence began with Hood, Rivera suggesting color for the murals, so that the big deep space at the bottom of a tall building wouldn't look like a crypt; Hood thought it should be in monochrome.

They were both obstinate men, and Nelson Rockefeller remained the mediator: the result was earth colors, reds, browns and greens. "The Battle of Rockefeller Center," however, developed over the subject matter.

In a general theme of "New Frontiers," Sert had been given the subject of stamping out War, Bondage and Disease, and the development of the power to Conserve Life—in four murals. Brangwyn was concerned with the ethical development of mankind, culminating in the Sermon on the Mount. Rivera's subject was man's new relation to matter and his new relation to man—himself; the preliminary sketch depicted three themes: man as the peasant developing the earth, the worker transforming and distributing the provisions of nature and the soldier, representing sacrifice.

Because he had undertaken a painting for the capitalists in the first place, Rivera was under pressure from the Communist Party, and not unnaturally he was anxious to show how good a Communist he really was. It was clear the sketch was a denunciation of capitalism, but on the other hand, the Rockefellers knew the personality of the artist, his ideas and his dedication to revolution.

They could well expect an honest expression of himself, and decided to take the chance in any case. On Nov. 7, 1932, Raymond Hood telegraphed Rivera, "Sketch approved by Nelson Rockefeller. Go right ahead with the large scale." Rivera started work on the job in March of 1933. While he had assistants to help with the layout and the mixing of materials he was upon the scaffold doing every inch of the nearly 1100 square feet of fresco painting himself. The mural was due for completion on May first, and as it progressed red banners appeared: "May Day in Communist Land," while further scenes illustrated a decadent civilization revolving about night clubs. Worst of all, the picture of the labor leader holding the hand of the peasant and the soldier took on the likeness of Lenin.

The cat was soon out of the bag: that Rockefeller was footing the bill for a Communist painting was soon in the headlines. Once more, Nelson Rockefeller tried to come to the rescue. As a work of art everything Rivera was doing was fine, but in his letter of May 4th Rockefeller wrote he was afraid the introduction of the head of Lenin might give offense and asked someone else be substituted. Rivera replied that the head of Lenin was in the original sketch in the hands of Raymond Hood.

Maybe it was, but not in the key position. And if elsewhere, it was unnoticed. Rivera further wrote, "I should prefer the physical destruction of the conception in its entirely, but preserving, at least its integrity." As a concession, he offered to add a picture of Lincoln. There was no compromise; Mr. Robertson ordered the work stopped, the fresco was covered with a canvas, and the artist paid in full.

The battle to save the painting was on; strangely the Communist Party itself remained silent. Regardless of whether or not his patron was a capitalist, Rivera felt he had an artist's right to do his work as he saw it. Rivera argued that if a capitalist were to buy the Sistine Chapel, would it give him the right to destroy the murals? Does an individual owner have the right to destroy what belongs to humanity at large? In spite of these powerful words, six months later the murals were pounded into dust, on February 9, 1934.

Will Rogers summed up the whole tragic episode this way: "I string with Rockefeller. This artist was selling some art and sneaking in some propaganda. Rockefeller had ordered a plain ham sandwich, but the cook put some onion in it. Rockefeller says, 'I will pay you for it, but I won't eat the onions.'"

Either man might have found a solution on his own that was mutually acceptable, but neither one could free himself from the bonds of his public image, one as the champion of Communism and the other of capitalism. The principles themselves triumphed. A year later the walls were re-covered with monochromatic murals by Jose Maria Sert. As far as Rivera was concerned, nobody would look at them.

Roxy and the Red Seats

When the RKO Theatre interests became an active part of the Rockefeller Center Project, Roxy was the leading figure. A short man of dynamic energy, he had the Napoleonic determination that seems to go with some people who are not as tall as those around them. The name Radio City, which became the colloquial name for Rockefeller Center, was first used in referring to Roxy's part of the enterprise, which included the NBC.

From the architectural point of view, Roxy's big contribution was the size and type of the Radio City Music Hall. To insist on a 6,000 seat auditorium with loudspeakers in the state of development they were in those days took a lot of courage, even though it was switching away from the concept of an opera house to the new one of "flesh shows."

The earlier Metropolitan Square project had been based on having an opera house as the heart of the project with, at the most, 3,500 seats. An opera house scheme usually contemplates a large ground floor, or orchestra, with horseshoe tiers or boxes above. With 6,000 seats, this system would not work accoustically in size nor arrangement, so as large an orchestra floor as possible was proposed with a huge balcony projecting out over the orchestra, perhaps a third of the way, and a shallow second balcony above. This would put a great number of seats under the low balcony ceiling, hidden from those above. When Roxy saw the plan he said no: the audience would be split into two or three groups, out of sight and sound of each other. He said unless you have a place where the people "laugh and cry together," you haven't got a theatre.

So the main floor was stretched to the acoustic limit as far as size was concerned and the balcony divided into three shallow tiers so people would not be underneath a great overhang and could look out over the heads of as many below as possible. As a result, the Music Hall became the great showplace for the kind of entertainment for which it was designed, despite all the gossip that it would not succeed. Not too much was said about what you could see in such a big hall, but the story has it that on opening night, one lucky holder of a ticket in the back row of the balcony said to another, "What are those little white mice doing down on the stage?"

"Mice?" was the reply. "Those aren't mice. Those are horses!" Shows had to be designed for the theatre.

Model for Radio City Music Hall, May 1931.   *courtesy of the author*

Roxy was equally dogmatic when it came to how the theatre should be furnished. The seating, of course was a major element, and a great number of sample seats of all kinds and sizes were gathered together, furnished in materials of all reasonable kinds and colors. Theatre seats have to stand a lot of wear and tear and have to be easily cleaned.

The color scheme came under discussion first: should the seats be blue, or maybe a handsome green? Roxy was adamant; he said the color was red and there was no use wasting time talking about any other possibility. In fact, he didn't know of one theatre that was a success that did not have red seats. And that was that.

Then came the question of what particular kind of a seat it should be, and all types were represented, both conventional and modern. One was a horror, upholstered, as I remember, with a series of little bolsters laid across the seat and up the back. Roxy headed for this, planked himself down and said, "This is it. I know." Various members of his staff pleaded with him that all the little crevices between the bolsters would be almost impossible to keep clean with one pass of the vacuum cleaner; the joints would collect everything, including bugs. They reasoned in vain.

Then others added, "It's too complicated, it would cost more, it would be difficult to repair. It's not as if it were just one seat; there are so many." No use; Roxy said that no matter what the troubles were, the design was worth it. At this point the delicate suggestion was made that maybe it was a perfect fit for a dynamic little Mr. Roxy, but surely not for the average person. Roxy's response was that he had sat in a lot of seats in his time and he knew a good one when he sat in it.

It looked as though the battle was lost. This time the biographer has to take the credit; I sidled up to Mr. Hood and suggested an answer in a low voice. Mr. Hood took over with, "Mr. Roxy, tell me, in all your experience, have you ever heard of a theatre that was a success that had seats like that?" Roxy flushed and said nothing more. The Music Hall went ahead with the best of the more conventional seats, certainly more comfortable than anything the New York theatre had had in a long time.

The Automatic Garage

It wasn't always a case of the architect putting over his own ideas; sometimes it was one of stopping those of other people. While Todd and Brown worked between the architects and the construction job, this didn't mean for one second they considered their position inferior in the hierarchy. Quite the contrary, they were ready to step in and straighten out the architects any time. Even if one of the best and most experienced of the old time draftsmen was laying out the lettering for the cornerstone, Joe (J.O.) Brown wouldn't hesitate to tell him he had the wrong kind of letters. Brown would then pick out a plate of lettering from somewhere else in the book and tell the expert to use that.

The color schemes certainly couldn't be left to the architects; as soon as he got word that a color scheme was being worked out, Joe Brown would appear. Whether the scheme was based on red, white or blue, Brown would explain the first rule: "It shouldn't show the dirt." The second rule was that the color be one that would be stocked in the building supply room. To help pick out such a color, Brown would open up the book of color tables and turn to one well thumbed page. "This," he said, "is what you're trying for." It was always the same color, earning the name of "Joe" brown.

Brown might have been right at that; years later when various publications were writing up their particular interests in the trade magazines the

> "With modern coming to the fore, it is felt brown will become even more important—underfoot. Already the floor coverings of Radio City have shown a tendency to this color in its range of hues."

Todd and Brown also had big ideas. One day there was a great bustle and commotion and Joe Brown appeared with an assembly of engineers, salesmen, catalogs, and diagrams. The idea was to have a parking garage. Nobody questioned that the difficulties of parking would be more serious in the neighborhood after Radio City was completed than before; in those days, however, it did not cause much concern. What would now be considered essential was then merely desirable if economically justified. The type of parking garage with ramps was already well established, but ramps took up a lot of space and the ratio of the net usable, or rentable, areas to the gross was very low compared to that of office buildings.

With high priced land like Radio City, the garage couldn't compete. Then a man appeared with a patented idea for a parking garage far more efficient than anything to date. The net to gross ratio was so high, in fact, that it seemed possible of consideration even for Radio City. In any event, the man was able to convince Joe Brown of the merits of the scheme. There was still a portion of the site unassigned and it didn't take more than a few calculations to show that a garage of this type would fit. They all gathered up the plans and came down to see the architects about putting the garage into the scheme. While a garage wasn't quite the kind of tenant the architects had anticipated for the site, if the scheme worked it would be hard to say no.

The plans were unfolded in front of Hood, who, if not quite sympathetic, was ready to listen. It was explained that the idea worked on the principle of a great turntable, in the middle of which there was an elevator large enough to take a car. All around the perimeter of the turntable were spaces to park cars. After bringing up an automobile, the attendants would push it out onto the turntable, which was successively rotated until all the outer spaces were filled. All the spaces on the turntable would be filled but one, which would be necessary in order to remove any particular car. Since there could be any reasonable number of floors, these floor plans seemed to reflect the greatest possible number of parking spaces, compared to the usual ramp type garage. Joe Brown said the scheme looked good to him and as far as he was concerned it could go into the plans.

134

Hood was quicker with figures than anyone I have ever known. "Well, Joe," Hood began diplomatically, "that certainly seems like a swell idea. It beats anything I've seen yet. But before we put it on the plans I want to be sure I've got everything straight."

Hood went into the details: "How long would it take to put a car away with this elevator? Three minutes, you say? Well, assuming the building holds two hundred cars, that would take six hundred minutes—ten hours. In other words, the tenants begin arriving at eight o'clock in the morning and by the time the first are ready to go home they would still be trying to park arriving tenants backed up all day goodness knows how many blocks down the street. I tell you, Joe, this may be all right on the plains of Kansas, but it's not for Radio City."

So the garage was out, for the time being. Years later, in 1939, the Eastern Airlines Building was built on the site that had been held for the Opera in case it could ever come back into the scheme. Including the street floor there were six stories of modern parking garage in the building, two above grade and three below or a total of eight hundred parking spaces. A home run this time for J.O. and a great convenience to the tenants.

Another Kind of Office

If for Raymond Hood, working as one of a team of architects, Radio City was to be a new experience, for the handful of us who came over from 40 West 40th Street, it was to be a new experience in what an architect's office could be like. In the first place, it was much larger, perhaps ninety people all told at its height. The atmosphere, too, was quite different; it was the depth of the Depression and we were among the lucky few to have a job at all. We did not forget for a minute that if we didn't always like the way things were done there were plenty more outside the door who would be more than pleased to put up with anything if they could have our job.

If there was any system in the office of Raymond Hood at 40 West 40th Street it was hard to detect. You were on your own to do whatever was necessary to get the job done. Nobody made you work, or even paid overtime for it; you sat up nights because you wanted to put in all the time necessary to get results. Once somebody told Raymond Hood he should hire an efficiency expert to put some system into his office. So he did. But when he found him checking the time cards of the draftsmen he promptly fired him. There are other values.

Now everything was order and efficiency, run by the clock. Draftsmen signed in at 8:30 A.M. and out at 5:30 P.M. Then the door was locked. If extra work was necessary, it would be authorized and paid for. That there could be any voluntary work was inconceivable. Despite the locked doors, though, just as in the good old days before the Crash, if there was work that we felt had to be done in time for morning meeting somehow it always was. As far as I know, they never found out that some of us had a duplicate key hidden in the mail slot of the drafting room door.

For a job the size of Radio City the system was a good thing; in Hood's office, if you needed a manufacturer's shop drawing you poked around until you found it half buried in a mess of papers on somebody's table. Here there was a battery of drawers behind a long counter and two or three office boys under the capable direction of Mr. Butler. If the drawing you wanted didn't pop out of the file in seconds, in minutes the office boys found there was hell to pay.

When the new office opened at 420 Lexington Avenue, some eight or ten draftsmen in all came together from the three offices. I remember the drafting room seemed a mile long after Hood's office; there were two rows of boards along the windows and another row across the aisle on the inside, all the same size and height with matching stools. Each had a T-square precisely set on the board and an ash tray in the upper right hand corner.

With all the boards alike, there was not much choice in making yourself at home, and we settled down. One of our number was Ralph Calder, a distinguished designer, a marvelous draftsman, as well as an artist well known for his beautiful illustrations. He was a short man, and the new boards and stools were too high for him. To get one adjusted to his size, he had the office boy saw off the legs of the drafting horses and the stool as well, so that he would be at the height to which he was accustomed.

While we were out to lunch, the head draftsman came in to look around. Something was wrong; in the middle of his plateau of precisely aligned drafting tables there was a depression. One of the boards was lower than the rest. He resolved the situation by sending out for another saw and putting the two available office boys to work cutting down all the tables and drafting stool legs in the entire row. They would all be one height once more, from one end of the room to another. When we came back, we knew that times had changed.

If John R. Todd was the iron man to the office, to salesmen he was a terror. With the Depression closing in and this Radio City job the only ongoing project, anyone having anything to sell in the way of building materials came to Todd's door. I was there one day when he was lambasting a salesman for wasting his time trying to pass off "a worthless good-for-nothing piece of junk."

136   Instead of crawling out of the room, browbeaten and defeated, the salesman flew back with, "my product isn't worthless, good-for-nothing junk." According to him, it was good stuff, what the project needed. To my surprise John R. Todd melted into a kindly affable gentleman, with a "sit down and tell me more about it."

Todd explained, after the man had left, that he was besieged all day by people trying to put something over on him, and he gave them the works, in self defense. If they were trying to put something over on him they collapsed under the blast and departed with their tails between their legs, but if they were sincere they flared back at him. Then Mr. Todd, who was the first to appreciate a good product or an idea properly explained, was ready to listen with a smile.

On another occasion I was busy inking the working drawings on cloth when Mr. Hood came by and saw something he wanted to change. George Johnston, the head draftsman, hurried over with, "You can't change that, Mr. Hood. These drawings are in ink!"

"How long have you been in this business? Thirty years? And you think a drawing can't be changed because it's in ink?"

This reminded me of the young man who had had to go out and measure the steel on the American Radiator Building when it was already under construction, so Mr. Hood could make one more change. Mr. Johnston's theory you couldn't change a working drawing after it was in ink literally came down in a cloud of eraser dust. The drawings of Buildings No. 1 and No. 9, or the RCA Building were now substantially completed, laid out on the assumption that steam would be supplied from the street by the New York Street Steam Corp. This would save the owner having his own boiler room and heating plant, no small item in a seventy story building.

When the management came to negotiate the contract for the steam, the price of steam had gone up despite the Depression, up substantially. Negotiations were put off for a week; with no alternative to using street steam, the steam corporation thought it had Radio City over a barrel.

Word came down to the drafting room to be prepared to work overtime, including the weekend. The engineers redesigned the basement to include a boiler room of huge capacity, finding room for it by pushing the floor down to sixty feet below the street in bedrock. More critical in the plans was the addition of a huge flue requiring a masonry enclosure, a space of fourteen by sixteen feet, all the way up through the building for seventy stories.

The core of the building had already been laid out in a tight package of stairs, elevators, toilets, and pipe shafts; the inclusion of the flue space meant a lot of plans would have to be changed. The order went out for electrical erasers, the first some of us had ever seen, and all hands were put to work rubbing out the heart of the building and redrawing it with a boiler room and an adequate flue from basement to roof. At the next meeting with the steam corporation, the revised drawings were lying on the table for all to see, complete with boiler room and flue, if anybody was interested. Nothing was said, but the price of steam went down.

Though the office worked under constant pressure, there were ways of relieving the tension. On the inside wall of the drafting room was a small wash basin enclosed with a couple of pieces of office partitioning, the upper half of one of them without glass so you could lean out. Every once in a while, about midafternoon, things would build up and somebody would say, "Well, Doc, start the train." "Doc" was the nickname I had acquired, probably because of the old black bag I carried with me on odd assignments. Amongst other things, I had a little whistle and a horn, which were used to start a French train, and I knew the part. I would go over to the little cubicle with the wash basin, lean out the window and blow my whistle and toot my horn with as much rumpus as possible, calling out, "En place, Messieurs, en place."

Called to start the train one afternoon, I went to the cubicle and did my little whistle and horn act. From the little window, it was evident all were drawing lines as intensely and grimly as possible. So I leaned out of the cab a little further to take a look down the track.

The cause of the silence and devotion to duty became apparent: Reinhard and Hofmeister had taken this moment to show off the drafting room to John D. Rockefeller, Jr., and as far as I know it was the first and last time he ever came in to have a look.

Who Built Radio City?

As the project neared completion, it was turning out a lot better than people had been led to believe by the newspapers; in fact as time went on, more and more individuals began to identify themselves as responsible for the success of the project. One editorial in the *New York Times* went so far as to imply that with the coming of the great projects like Radio City, the ordinary run of architects and engineers were finding themselves unable to cope with the manifold and complex problems, far beyond anything in their experience. According to the *Times* editorial, these experts in their fields were finding that some sort of super individual was necessary to coordinate and organize their work, a man of great imagination, organizational ability and understanding. Such a man, it stated, was Donald Desky.

138

Now Donald Desky was a fine man, who had recently come out of the Navy. It had been decided to hold a competition for designing the interior finishes and furnishings of the various public rooms in the two theatres, including the estimates of the cost for doing the work. Desky won the competition for doing the interiors connected with the big Music Hall with his good, economical job. He achieved much individuality in the various settings by bringing in the work of various artists and artisans, many of whom lived in Greenwich Village.

However, it was news that Desky was the new leader pulling together the work of the floundering architects and engineers. Even if it were true, it was a little late in the game to carry out such lofty ambitions. As far as the plans were concerned, they were all done. The theatres were planned to meet the requirements of Roxy and the RKO and they had been designed in the office, which made it interesting for me to read an article in *Variety* written about Roxy. When asked how he conceived the idea of the great theatres, he said, "I didn't conceive the idea, I dreamed it. I believe in creative dreams. The picture of the Radio City theatres was complete and practically perfect in my mind before architects and artists put pen to the drawing paper." Elsewhere he said his inspiration came "from watching the sunrise at sea." It could have been—on his way home to bed.

Pictures of more and more people began to appear as the man of the hour in Radio City. One day we were passing the Fifth Avenue window of one of the noted portrait photographers and Hood noted another portrait in the gallery. Hood thought he'd had a lot to do with Radio City too, but nobody ever put his picture in the window on Fifth Avenue. "Don't worry," I answered, "The windows may be full of pictures of people who designed Radio City, and the Sunday Magazines full of stories. However, if somebody who really cares takes a look at the *Daily News* Building and the RCA Building from comparable angles, they will *know* who designed Radio City."

The Site

Most of us working in the office under constant pressure had little time to think about the significance of what we were doing. Still, it was more than just another job; it was just about the only one going ahead in the Depression. I saw it as a unique opportunity to gain experience and worked in all the various capacities I could. During my lunch hour, I took a 16mm motion picture of the progressive developments of the project; this also gave me the chance to follow the construction of the job in the field.

The main inspiration for this movie was a clipping my father sent me

The RCA Building.
                    courtesy of author

New York Daily News Building.
                    courtesy of the author

COMPARATIVE PLANS

Note: Not to same scale

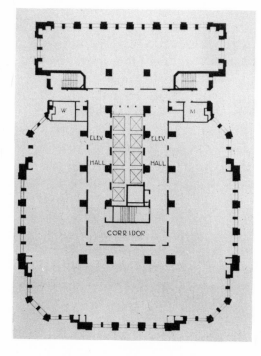

Chicago Tribune, 1922

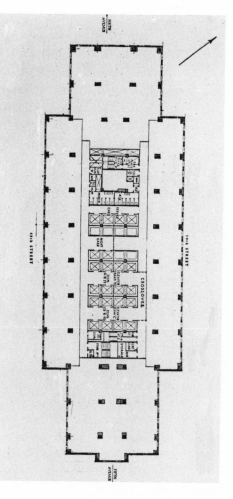

American Radiator, 1924

Rockefeller Center, R.C.A. Bld., 1933

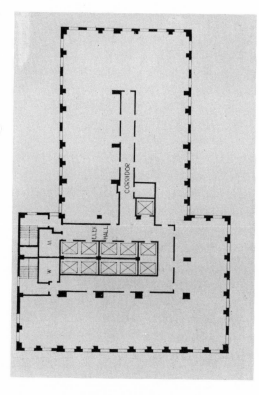

Daily News, 1930

from a Boston newspaper; it contained a few comments by the noted Boston architect Ralph Adams Cram. While in Cram's opinion the world had never achieved anything greater than the Thirteenth Century English Gothic, he conceded that America had made a unique contribution to architecture in the skyscraper. It started with the Woolworth Building, and Cram cited its culmination in the Empire State Building. Cram's thesis pointed to the proposed design of the RCA Building as a further development, the decline and fall of the art: "And its Nemesis, Radio City, for such it certainly is. . . ." If this was to be the last of the skyscrapers, it seemed up to me to try to record these last days on film.

The results of a little research into the origin of the great enterprise and history of the site may be of interest. It actually started with an attempt to find a new home for the Metropolitan Opera. The Met had moved a number of times since it was founded; once again the desirable neighborhood had changed, and the building, now forty-three years old, had become antiquated and short of space. In January, 1926, Otto Kahn, Chairman of the Board of the Opera undertook to find a new site.

While it was hoped that the location be in or adjacent to the theatre district, it was essential to the patrons that it be readily accessible to the "carriage trade" that supported the Opera. But they found that any site in the theatre district was financially out of reach due to competition. It was not until February 1927 that Mr. Kahn located a piece of property on 57th Street between Eighth and Ninth Avenues.

This property was not ideal but it was the best Kahn could afford. Benjamin Wistar Morris was retained as the architect to draw up the plans. Joseph Urban, architect of the well known Ziegfeld Theatre, who had come over from Austria and established himself as a leading designer of stage sets for the Opera, made a separate submission on his own and was later retained as consultant. Urban was one of Raymond Hood's best friends from his early days in New York.

As the plans developed, so did the feeling of "society" who would be the box-holders, against the location. They saw it as an undesirable neighborhood for the Opera, and the project for the new Opera was received with little enthusiasm. The period was one of increasing prosperity, but the future of an opera house dependent on private financial support did not seem too bright. And the modicum of office-studio space which the 57th Street project included with the object of earning some commercial revenue, was destined to grow in future schemes. Although hardly realized at the time this commercial aspect was to prove fatal to the new Opera project.

On 63rd Street, a slightly better site was found and new plans were prepared and estimated. Even more revenue was required with the higher land values, and the proportion of office-studio space was increased; the results were again unsatisfactory. Then an important location became available on Columbus Circle, and Benjamin Wistar Morris again prepared plans. On this site, there was more room and the Opera would have an important and distinctive outlook for both theatre and business in an urban focal point.

Rentals would be higher, but the investment would be far greater because of the increased values of real estate involved. The handwriting was on the wall: the indicated amount of commercial space became an overshadowing feature in the mass of the project compared to the size of the Opera. Concerned, Morris wrote to R. Fulton Cutting, the President of the Metropolitan Opera and Real Estate Company, that even with the higher rentals the Opera would require an "endowment fund of large dimensions."

The outlook for the new Opera house was still far from encouraging. Morris also suggested a location on the downtown property of Columbia University, which was not considered further at the time because it was understood that this land, or any part thereof, would only be leased, not sold. And the Opera was interested only in the purchase of a site. Then in January 1928 came an entirely new possibility for the Columbia University property that comprised the major part of three blocks between Fifth and Sixth Avenues in Midtown. Leases on various parcels would begin to expire in 1928, and it occurred to Tonelle of William A. White and Sons, who were real estate consultants to both the Opera and Columbia, that a portion of the south block, in from the Sixth Avenue Corner, could become available to the Opera at a reasonable cost.

The area was a run-down neighborhood full of speakeasies and even less desirable tenants referred to as "ladies of the evening." It would be to the economic interest of the University to bring in an enterprise that would improve the character of the property.

To make up for the lack of important frontage, since neither the Fifth Avenue—St. Nicholas Church or Sixth Avenue frontages were controlled by the University, Tonelle had in mind constructing a private street from 48th to 49th Streets. He took his idea to Mr. Cutting, who asked him to see what could be done on this new site, since it was the best location so far from the social viewpoint although not a solution of the economic question. Morris wrote in a letter of February 12, 1928, that "while this scheme did not help materially in a financial way, it fathered my thought that if carried further it might show us a way out of our difficulties."

This "way out" Morris saw as taking over Columbia's holdings in all three blocks, as required, running the sixty-foot private street all the way through to 51st Street. A great plaza could be developed in the center block, to be a distinguished location in the city, a "City within a City" lending value and prestige to the commercial developments that could be built around it. The resultant revenue might be enough to carry both the enterprise and the Opera.

Prospects for city planning on a large scale appeared for the first time in a New York commercial development. In this "big idea" the commercial aspects which would make the project financially feasible would dominate, but allow the Opera to have a monumental site on a distinguished plaza.

The large site had an interesting history leading up to its availability under one ownership. It was first acquired, as such, by Dr. David Husack, a physician of reputation and a professor of botany and materia medica at Columbia College. Unable to get state support for a botanical garden he had in mind to create, he undertook to finance it himself. Husack found an adequate tract of public land of some twenty acres on Middle Road, the future Fifth Avenue. Rough, stony and wooded, it was considered unsuitable for farm land but suited the purpose of Dr. Husack.

In 1801 Dr. Husack leased the property, and at great personal expense laid out and planted with trees and shrubs the Elgin Botanical Garden, one of the wonders of New York at the time. He was a founder of the College of Physicians and Surgeons and after 1807 was bringing his medical students to his garden, which included medicinal herbs. By 1810 he had acquired the land from the city for something over $5,000, but successful as the project became it was soon beyond his means to support. The state agreed to buy it for approximately $75,000 "for the benefit of the medical schools of the state."

The state, however, was not willing to do anything to maintain this valuable garden, and in 1814 a number of colleges were petitioning the state for aid, one of these Columbia College on Park Place. The state saw an opportunity to unload the garden instead of the money Columbia was seeking. The Botanic Garden would be granted and vested in the Trustees of Columbia College, provided they locate the College on the property within twelve years. This grant however was not considered "an attractive or helpful gift" by the trustees.

The land became known as the "Upper Estate" to distinguish it from the property on Park Place, and it was not until 1823 that Columbia was able to collect any rent on the property, $125 a year. The first indicated subdivision of the property appeared on the city map showing the system of numbered streets and avenues in use today. Forty-eighth, Forty-ninth, Fiftieth, and Fifty-first streets traversed the garden, and Middle Road became Fifth Avenue and the westerly Albany Road became Sixth Avenue. Various restrictions on the property were removed in 1819 and Columbia College was free to sell or lease, but the total value of only $7,500 at the time was hardly worth selling.

In 1828, the first twenty-one year lease was made to a farmer at $400 a year. He too had to give up in the face of many difficulties and in 1833 his lease was assigned to a creditor. This man, John Ward, foresaw the trend of the time and planned to subdivide the property into house lots. Columbia realized this change into a subdivision would be worth $46,000 a year in rent, whereas John Ward was only paying $350. The subdivision did not take place.

The property, now called Elgin Grove, rapidly deteriorated. The first cross street was opened in 1841. By 1850 the property was heavily in debt, and a committee of the Trustees were ready to sell the future site of Rockefeller Center. However, the courageous Board felt otherwise and decided to proceed with the plan of subdivision. By 1856 they had already abandoned the idea of building a new Columbia College on the property as too expensive; they acquired the old Deaf and Dumb Asylum a block away on Madison Avenue and the college was located there for the next forty years.

The garden property was now worth $550,000, and the college still needed money; this time the trustees couldn't resist selling sixteen lots on Fifth Avenue to the Dutch Reformed Church for $40,000. The rest of the property was divided into 272 lots, which were all leased by 1869, and from then on the policy of leaseholds only was adhered to. This policy was no doubt confirmed by the neat profit the church made of $77,000 by selling half their lots for the sum of $117,000.

Another aspect of the leasehold policy is seen in the report of the Finance Committee in 1888 concerning "Leases on the Upper Estate." It referred to an action of the Trustees in or about 1857 on making

> ". . . concessions to tenants . . . one of the constituent elements of value, so far as the lots on the side streets at least are concerned, in the opinion of the lessees and many disinterested persons well qualified to judge, lies in the fact that the use of the property is limited to dwelling purposes and may be controlled.
>
> "If we revert to the character of the occupancy of properties held by lessees under leases containing only the ordinary covenants against nuisances, we may find in various portions of the city uses detrimental not only to the values, from the standpoint of both lessors and lessees, but also detrimental to good morals and decency."

In thinking of control, as in the key phrase above, the Committee was thinking of a tenancy of the genteel and affluent. Again not without good reason. According to an account by Claire Klein of "The Rockefeller Center Property," the trustees'

> ". . . general resolution to be selective might well have been rein-forced by the object lesson afforded in a lot on the corner of 52nd Street, near the Columbia property, which was owned and occupied by Madam Restill, the notorious abortionist and central figure in a sensational mur-der trial. Her purchase of the lot through an agent caused such a de-preciation of nearby land value that a contemporary gossip reported that lots have been offered—at one quarter of what those on the next block have brought but there are no takers."

What the worthy trustees would have thought of their "controlled" occupancy in the 1920's is not hard to imagine. As the demolition for Rockefeller Center commenced, contemporary gossip of the day was to say Rockefeller was destroying two hundred old brownstones and "a thousand speakeasies." For the comfort of the trustees of Columbia we must hasten to point out that it was not their lessees that had been beyond control, but their sub-tenants.

It was important for the project of the new opera house that the property was still in one ownership, generally in leaseholds that would expire in good time, and the plan was rapidly developed. The completed drawings were exhibited to a distinguished gathering of leading citizens at the Metro-politan Club on May 21st, 1928. For the first time, a commercial base for the venture seemed reasonable; several more ideas in this "Metropolitan Club" scheme were notable.

As Morris pointed out, under the zoning law, much greater heights of two hundred to two hundred fifty feet fronting on the plaza would be per-mitted, as compared with those of ninety feet on sixty-foot streets. This meant increased revenues, more than offsetting the value of the land left open on the plaza. Another consideration was that the acquisition of the space for the Plaza and its development could be through private subscrip-tions, the whole to be donated to the city on completion.

Great enthusiasm greeted this plan; at last there was a scheme that would seem to pay its way and help the Opera too. In return for a monu-mental setting in a desirable and convenient neighborhood, the Opera would contribute the prestige essential to the overall success of the enter-prise and create a valuable shopping and business center. A haunting shadow, though, still remained.

Originally, Mr. Kahn had set out to find a site for an Opera House, within an enterprise the Opera Company could reasonably undertake on its own, but the plan had grown to an enormous civic development far beyond anything they ever had in mind. Still, luck seemed to be with them; present in the distinguished assembly at the Metropolitan Club that night were representatives of John D. Rockefeller, Jr. The idea was brought back to him; he became enthusiastic and soon found he was ready to undertake the entire enterprise on his own as a great civic development with a cultural focus, the Opera, for which a site would be provided.

Based on the plan of Benjamin Wistar Morris, Rockefeller founded the Metropolitan Square Corporation, and in January 1929, President Butler of Columbia announced that this new corporation would take over the entire leasehold of the properties which the University controlled in the three blocks and would pay an annual rental. This was the high point of the Opera's prospects.

Rendering of Metropolitan Square with Opera, by Benjamin Wistar Morris.
courtesy of R. B. O'Connor

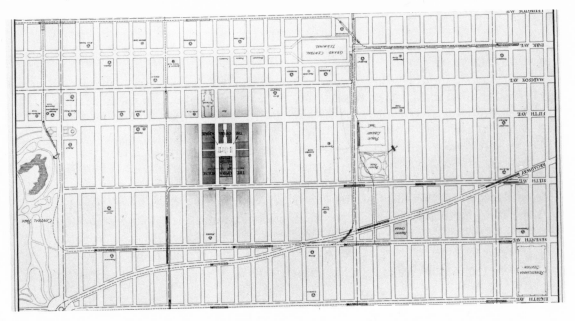

Proposed site for Metropolitan Opera House.   *courtesy of R. B. O'Connor*

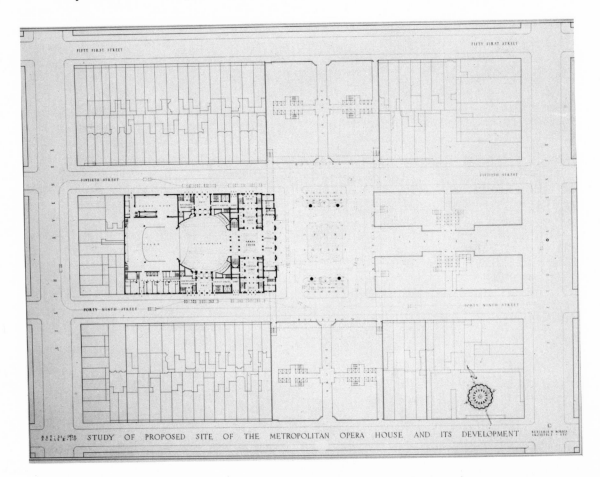

Plan for Metropolitan Square, May 21, 1928, by Benjamin Wistar Morris.
courtesy of R. B. O'Connor

From Opera House to "Oil Can City"

Once Rockefeller had decided he was ready to take over the whole enterprise and had completed arrangements with Columbia University, he realized the architectural considerations would now extend far beyond the original development of the Opera House alone, and would involve urban planning on a large scale.

In order to review the Metropolitan Club proposal in view of the new development Rockefeller invited some eight or ten firms of well known architects, including Benjamin Wistar Morris representing the Opera, to come up with their best suggestions. Morris further developed his idea for a broad promenade from Fifth Avenue on the axis of the Opera, flanked on either side by tall buildings. Eventually they were modified by low six story buildings.

On the up- and downtown sides, the Plaza was to be surrounded by revenue producing buildings some ten stories high, which were now continued westward with additional towers at the Sixth Avenue corners of the site. Now included in the project were the entire holdings of Columbia in the three blocks; according to the drawing the acquisition of the entire three blocks including St. Nicholas Church on Fifth Avenue was assumed. Corbett, Harrison and MacMurray submitted a complete scheme which also introduced the idea of a promenade from Fifth Avenue, but it would be graded up to a second story level grand entrance to the Opera. This would connect with upper level shopping promenades that were already part of Morris' original scheme. Still, Morris' original project as the basis of procedure remained basically the same, although the overall scheme benefited by the discussions. For further development, it was sent down to the office of John D. Rockefeller.

All the leases from Columbia University would be taken over by the newly-formed Metropolitan Square Corporation, and special provision would be made to reserve a proper site for the Opera, to be carried by the Opera company. Rockefeller was experienced in the oil business, but felt more expert advice was needed. He had consulted in the interim with five New York real estate companies and in particular with John R. Todd, who was a well known contractor with wide interests and experience in the building field.

As a result of a discussion at Rockefeller's summer home in Seal Harbor in the summer of 1929, John R. Todd was appointed to carry out the project, and Todd had his young architects Reinhart and Hofmeister draw up a new plan for Metropolitan Square, the Opera House and Plaza scheme of Morris, dated Labor Day of that year. In accordance with Todd's directions it indicated hotels on either side of the plaza and an office building tower on the westerly corners as his initial suggestion for the commercial development, the esplanade from Fifth Avenue to the square to be retained but with two low buildings either side.

To manage the enterprise, Todd reorganized his firms of Todd, Robertson and Todd; Todd Engineering Corp.; and Todd and Brown in the meantime, which became Todd, Robertson and Todd, Todd and Brown, and was announced to the press on Oct. 5th of the year. To the reporters' queries, Todd gave no answer whether Benjamin Wistar Morris would be the architect, but he did say "the final plans will not differ radically from those prepared by Mr. Morris." On the 25th of October, Todd appointed the firm who had been doing work for his office, Reinhard and Hofmeister, as architects, and named Benjamin Wistar Morris, Raymond Hood and Harvey Corbett as consultants.

Mr. Todd's comment in a news bulletin was that "the work of these men, particularly the consultants, is very well known and requires no comment. It is however of interest that Mr. Morris is the architect of the new opera house, also that he is the first architect to propose placing the opera, with the plaza in front of it, in the center of the three blocks." The terms Todd proposed to Morris, however were unfortunately unacceptable to Morris, considering the background and knowledge he had to contribute to the project, not to mention the basic idea of development. Morris withdrew from the Metropolitan Square project in December.

While it was assumed the Opera would sign up for its part of the enterprise, the company hesitated. Whatever the underlying causes may have been, there was one good and sufficient reason for this. Nobody could put it into words better than Frederick Lewis Allen in the April, 1932 issue of *Harpers*. According to Allen, when Rockefeller had taken over the Columbia University leasehold for the entire property:

"... a large part of the tract had naturally already been leased by Columbia for varying terms of years to shopkeepers and small businesses, and some of the lessees had sublet to what the newspapers call alleged speakeasies. To gain possession it became necessary for Rockfeller's agents to buy up these leases. Now if there is one thing calculated to bring tears of joy to the eyes of a small business man, it is to hold a lease in a piece of property which is being assembled by John D. Rockefeller, Jr. A good many of the Columbia tenants exhibited a strange reluctance to vacate without suitable reimbursement, and their ideas of what would be suitable reimbursement became exalted. Mr. Rockefeller's representatives were adept at the poker-game of real estate purchasing, but there were leases in the property which could be acquired only by paying through the nose; and the estimated cost of the development began to mount disturbingly. Mr. Cutting and his associates of the Opera Company looked on uneasily—and did not sign."

When in the fall of '29 the Crash came, it soon became apparent the Opera would not be coming in for the present; in fact, it withdrew from the enterprise in December. Worse yet, the bottom was dropping out of all real estate values. Rockefeller, who had already agreed to buy out the old lessees at high prices, was responsible for the enormous taxes plus the $3,000,000 a year rental he now owed Columbia. With little coming in and the property undeveloped, it would be an understatement to say Rockefeller was left holding the bag.

It was no longer a case of developing a "cultural center" for the benefit of the Opera and the City, it was a case of finding some way to salvage the venture by any means possible. Rockefeller had vast resources but he could not see tens of millions of dollars going down the drain without finding a way to plug the leak. Although the "cultural" image persisted for a long time in the public mind, the project changed from a cultural project to a ruthlessly commercial one. The site plan of November 28, 1929 still showed the "Opera House"; the plan of January 8, 1930 shows it changed to "Major Building No. 1!"

It was at this stage that I began to work on the project in Raymond Hood's office. The first schemes we did indicated stores and shops, with ramps to the upper level streets with bridges over 49th and 51st Streets. The curious part is that Hood wanted to be able to have cars drive up, whereas I thought they should be for pedestrians only; this showed me as the "man on foot" at heart and Hood as the "man on wheels" although not without uncertainties. Don Hatch tells me that when he visited Hood on the weekends he always dreaded any rides with Hood as the driver, for, whenever they came to a crossroad, he would speed up and tear through. According to Hood, "Intersections are where the danger lies and you want to get through them as fast as you can."

Another of Hood's characteristics became evident one time after some kind of collision of fenders, when the irate driver leaped out, apparently ready to take Hood apart then and there. According to Hatch, it was typical of Hood that, after talking things over quietly a few minutes, his new "friend" followed him back to the house for a drink.

In the only reference I heard Hood make to Morris' original Opera scheme, he said the idea of walling in the Opera with high buildings like a "Forbidden City" was basically wrong. He felt that the Opera should not

151

be in a place separate from the rest of the city, but a place should open into it as an integral part. So with Metropolitan Square, if there must be a lot of commercial space, let it be concentrated in the center, looking out over low roofs in the north and south blocks. In this way the builders not only assure light and air for their project, but also for its neighbors, who may thus be encouraged to do likewise.

This is the way the plan for Rockefeller Center developed in principle, more naturally, though when the Opera House was changed to a commercial building. The offices of the consultants and Reinhard and Hofmeister combined in July, 1930 in one joint office in the Graybar Building, as Reinhard and Hofmeister, Corbett, Harrison and MacMurray, Raymond Hood, Godley and Fouilhoux. Once the three offices combined there was somewhat less chance of finding time to work out any better idea for the general plan; the overall lease was set and the problem clear: find a solution that would pay. As the full impact of the Depression became more apparent, the weight of the requirements became heavier; the basic problem was how to find enough rentable space on this site to pay off nearly $10,000,000 a year for rent, taxes and interest on the mortgage.

The numerous schemes were mostly variations on the original theme: a major office building in the center block with four smaller towers in the diagonal corners and low buildings in between, the variations consisting largely of combinations for the low buildings, stores, apartments, hotels, theaters, and more office or loft space. This was further modulated as additional pieces of property came under control, particularly along Sixth Avenue. Still, any solutions and assumptions as to the uses of space were hypothetical, for there were no prospective tenants.

Finally, there came a break: it was announced that the Radio Corporation of America, together with NBC, would come into the picture as the major tenant, closely followed by the RKO, and each had several affiliates with it. The program now came alive for the architects, with the inclusion of broadcasting studios, theaters, and related office spaces. With the theaters came Roxy, S.L. Rothafel of RKO. If a gap had been left in the high plane of the original enterprise, with the loss of the Opera, "Radio as an Art," and a huge "Variety Theater" leaped in to fill the space. So successfully, in fact, as far as publicity was concerned, that the *New York Times* was able to announce the revitalized project as "Rockefeller Plans Huge Culture Center" on the front page.

The theater district publication, *Variety*, was more down to earth. It saw the great Music Hall as "a two-a-day and limited to flesh shows." With all this came the nickname that stuck: Radio City, originally applied to the broadcasting and theatre development only, now at the west end of

First Exhibition Model of
Radio City, March 5, 1931.
courtesy of Frederick Bradley

the project. All these additions were quickly fitted into the framework of the basic scheme, but there were still large sites awaiting a purpose; a large one in the center of the south block was still reserved for the Opera, in case there should be any change that would make its entry possible once again.

Nearly a year went by, and at last the scheme was ready, the plasticine model cast in white plaster. In principle, the Benjamin Wistar Morris plan remained, with Buildings 1 and 9, to be known as the RCA Building, substituted for the Opera, but still with a Plaza, though smaller, in front, and connected to 48th and 51st Streets by private ways. The broad promenade from Fifth Avenue had been replaced by an oval building around which the crowd was supposed to flow, lead on by a succession of shop windows that

Critics' Viewpoint
courtesy of New York Evening
Journal

would lure them off the avenue. This idea was known as "a million dollars on the ground," and considered the best addition yet to the income side of the estimate, for the number of square feet involved.

A grand opening to view the plans was announced for March 5, 1931, to which all newsmen were invited. As a sort of jack of all trades, I was to see that not only was the model properly spotlighted but also that it revolved. To accomplish the latter I was sent over to borrow the portable automobile turntable from the Chrysler show room window across the street. Mr. Chrysler had been a client of Reinhard and Hofmeister and it seemed like a reasonable idea, except that once the model was set up we discovered the new Chrysler Building was on a.c. current and the old Grand Central Zone was on d.c. Nevertheless, everything was ready for the party in time, and a fine buffet set up. Everyone seemed to have a good time as the gleaminng white model slowly revolved against its background of velvet drapes.

In the office, we could hardly wait to read the morning papers. We were unprepared for the blast: if the dream of a "Culture City" was shattered, so were any hopes of an architectural achievement, at least in the opinions of the critics of the day that followed. The cartoonist depicted "The Oil Can City" with the RCA Building indicating a more than coincidental resemblance to a rectangular kerosene can. The treasured elliptical building was referred to as a gas tank. And this first step in multiple block urban development in the city was damned by Lewis Mumford, "Chaos does not have to be planned." The summation came in the editorial by Royal Cortissoz in the *Herald Tribune,* ending with the words, "The crux of the business is that Radio City is ugly."

The page of letters to the *Herald Tribune* that followed was entitled, "The Uprising Against Radio City." The first letter said, "We have seen beauty kicked in the face so often and so flagrantly by advocates of "Utility" —which word is usually a synonym for 'greed'. . . ." Later articles were to follow in the journals: Frank Lloyd Wright declared Radio City would probably be "the last atrocity committed upon a people already about to revolt . . ."; Ralph Adams Cram went even further: "then by all means let us see Radio City built as quickly as possible for the sooner we accomplish the destiny it so perfectly foreshadows, the sooner we shall be able to clear the ground and courageously begin again."

Only the *Daily News* stood by the ship:

> "In the News building Mr. Hood designed what is generally considered a beautiful building. He did it by producing a highly efficient newspaper plant and office building. Mr. Hood and the other architects on the Radio City job hope to apply the same principles to that project. They want to rear a group of buildings which will be first of all useful and efficient for the intended purposes and users. Looking at the model, we think that if left alone they will produce buildings useful and therefore beautiful. We're all for Hood and his crowd. . . ."

If the first effort had been to save the project from a financial disaster, the second was now to save it architecturally. After all this abuse, the drafting room was singularly quiet and determined, somehow imbued with a renewed purpose. If the emphasis had been to obtain the maximum number of rentable square feet for the volume available, now there seemed to be a little more appreciation, higher up, of what architecture meant after all. There was more use of plasticine models, and René Chambellan, the architectural sculptor, set up shop in the office so the designers could see their suggestions worked out in three dimensions. It gave the designers a chance to stand back a little and suggest a change here or another there, instead of being obliged to call for simply "more lines," the expression for putting heat on the draftsmen.

A good sketch of Raymond Hood as he appeared to others at this time comes down to us in this record of an interview; writing in the *New York Times Magazine* for November 1, 1931 in an article entitled "An Architect Hails the Rule of Reason," S.J. Woolf wrote:

> Because he is one of the three consultant architects for Radio City and has already completed a number of structures which have provoked much discussion, Raymond Hood has been compelled to stand the brunt of the criticism from those who cling to old ideas for new realities.

"There has been entirely too much talk," he said, "about the collaboration of architect, painter and sculptor; nowadays, the collaborators are the architects, the engineer and the plumber."

Mr. Woolf also described Hood as he appeared when interviewed in his 40th Street office:

He had on no coat or vest; his suspenders were hitched high and his ruffled soft collar was carelessly fastened about a drab-colored tie.

He is small and tanned, compact and full of energy. His dark eyebrows rise obliquely away from his nose and give him a perpetually surprised expression. This look is accentuated by his coarse, short-cropped gray hair, which stands up at an alarming angle from his head, as in one of those drawings by Cruikshank in the Ingoldsby Legends, of a man who has just seen a ghost.

But he is not the type to run from an apparition and material things do not frighten him. He has stood his ground against the violent onslaughts of those who have been most active in the fight for the preservation of what they believe are traditions.

Traditions, however, mean nothing to him except hurdles which must be jumped in order to keep pace with the fast tempo of modern life. In the New York buildings which were born on his drafting table he has disregarded old ideas: columns and capitals have been swept away and pilasters have given place to windows; splotches of color have given variety to unbroken surfaces. He has reared no temples to dead gods; he has built workshops for living men and in their construction he has proclaimed the era of business, of machinery and speed.

Woolf spoke of the period of opulence and extravagance that preceded the depression as reflected in the architecture of the period and thus:

Today the reverse is true. There is a straightforwardness and lack of ornamentation about our buildings that are the result not only of a desire for simplicity but also of our having to do things cheaply and retain good taste.

Woolf continued:

From architecture the conversation turned to painting and I mentioned a retrospective exhibition which I had visited and the disappointment I had experienced on seeing some paintings after a lapse of years. I wondered whether they had changed in color or whether it was I who had changed.

Hood had commented:

"I do not think that either changed. The point of view was different, I was born in Pawtucket and left there when I was a child. For years I carried around with me a memory of the mountains that surrounded the place. When I had grown up I revisited the neighborhood, and what was my surprise to find that the mountains had shrunk to little hills. My point of view had altered. The same thing is true in respect of art."

In conclusion Hood said:

"The new buildings which are being erected have a note of difference in them to which our eyes are not yet accustomed. We must become familiar with the new forms and then we shall see the beauty in them. When we do, then we shall look at the older buildings from a different standpoint and we shall be able to appreciate the beauties of both the old and the new."

The Final Plan Plus One for the Record

Following the press Exhibition of March 5th, 1931, there was little change in the overall plans for Radio City except the elimination of the oval building on Fifth Avenue and a return to the two low buildings flanking the esplanade from the avenue to the plaza. When he first took over, John R. Todd had stated after the central skyscraper had been substituted for the Opera, as recorded in the minutes of the Metropolitan Square Corporation on December 6th 1930, ". . . all planning of the square should be based upon 'a commercial center as beautiful as possible consistent with a maximum income that could be developed.' "

If there was a "Theme Song" for Radio City, this was it. An infinite number of schemes were tried out for the center but all within this search for an economic solution. In the end they all came back to the first plan of John R. Todd of December 6th, 1929 as drawn up by Reinhard and Hofmeister, which showed a central office tower with two smaller office buildings on the diagonals, and low department store and loft buildings in between. As such it remained but one step away from the original Opera scheme of Benjamin Wistar Morris.

At the time of the lease of the property, there remained a strip of buildings approximately one hundred feet wide along Sixth Avenue. With the cat out of the bag, there was no chance of acquiring this land at reasonable price. Without disclosing the least inkling of who was behind it, they had

157

a number of separate and unrelated purchasing agents set out to acquire the properties piecemeal. By the fall of 1930, they had substantially succeeded and the Metropolitan Square Corporation was able to add all the Sixth Avenue frontage to their site except for two corner lots.

All the studies were based upon hypothetical tenants, but upon the realization of contracts with RCA and RKO a final plan was reached and definite programs established for most of the sites on October 29th, 1931. In the interest of receiving a return on the investment as soon as possible, working drawings were pushed ahead for the first stage of construction; of the numbered sites on the basic plan this first stage now included: No. 1, and No. 9 as the RCA Building and NBC Studios; Nos. 2 and 3 the British and French Buildings with the esplanade between; No. 8 the Center Theater on the southwest corner; and building No. 10, the Radio City Music Hall with the RKO offices above the lobby on the northwest corner; Nos. 5, 6 and 7 were still open.

This plan was the collaborative effort of many interests besides the group of architects. The story of Hood's contributions has been told, leaving the conjecture as to what he, such an individualist, would have done had he been selected as the only architect. Record remains of what Raymond Hood had in mind when the three firms were working separately, bringing their plans together in the initial meetings with Mr. Todd. Hood's plans conform to the basic criterion of developing maximum income, and show a concentration of tall buildings in the center block looking out over low buildings to the north and south. They all ignore the original location of the plaza and generally show it on Fifth Avenue. Ramps are indicated to a second level of circulation with bridges over the streets. This was a common feature of all the architects' plans and was considered the only practical way to tie the three blocks into one development, still keeping the existing pattern of the through streets.

Once the three firms were combined in one organization they worked together on the various schemes. However, before the final conclusions were reached they were given a chance to come up with their own individual solution. There were no strings attached to this "architect's fling." Although some joint meetings did explode in an expression of personalities, each one storming out of the room, on the whole the architects had got along remarkably well. Thus we don't know for sure whether John R. Todd was hoping someone would come up with a better idea, or whether it was simply a safety valve for the architects working too long as one.

Hood worked up his scheme back in his own office. Photographs of the plans and models remain showing it as no longer a development covering three city blocks, dutifully recognizing the limitations of real estate parcels

"The Fling"—Model of Raymond Hood's Personal Scheme for Radio City.
courtesy of the author

not held. Rather, it is a single composition over the three block area and as such, is an architectural entity expressing the purpose of the component buildings. In massing the tall buildings towards the center, the final plan recognized Raymond Hood's basic concept that in a city, the mutual sharing of light and air over adjacent properties is as important to the entrepreneur as to his neighbors.

Beyond this the great advantage of the skyscraper to Hood was that it brought a lot of people together in one place, providing them with internal traffic circulation by elevators as compared with spreading out all over the adjacent streets for a mile or so. To further his idea, Hood's scheme shows the two parallel internal streets diverted to a cross pattern at the center. In this way the backs of the tall buildings comprising the scheme could be as close together as possible at the street level, comprising stairs, elevators and toilets which are not dependent upon natural light. By bringing them close together at the street level it would not only be easier to reach one or the other building from the outside, but by a lower basement level or bridge above it would be a shorter distance.

Above the street, wings of office space radiated from the central elevator core following the cross pattern of the street. These wings in each building embraced a space where low buildings like theatres or loft buildings could be built, without cutting off the light and air of the offices. In this the wings recalled Hood's early scheme for the Methodist temple in Columbus, Ohio.

Although it might have turned out quite differently, Radio City still turned out very well. Hood's scheme had an expression of order, unity and composition that was lacking in the model presented to the press and enlarged upon by critics. Once the architects had been given their chance to dream, they were called back to the task ahead, of getting the working drawings completed at all possible speed. Without waiting until they were finished with them, construction contracts were negotiated with three builders, the RCA Building going to Hegeman-Harris, the RKO Music Hall combination to John Lowry, Inc., and the two small Fifth Avenue buildings and Theatre No. 8 to Barr, Irons and Lane.

The final plan was dated April 1931, and progress photographs show demolition of the site under way by June 2nd. By July 31st, excavation had begun for the main skyscraper. Not all the required lots had been secured in advance and troubles developed; two strategic corner lots on Sixth Avenue were in this category. Unwilling to meet the hold-up terms of the owners, the management in the end decided to build around them for the present and hope to acquire them later on.

"Metropolitan Square," final model by Reinhart and Hofmeister; Corbett, Harrison and MacMurray; Raymond Hood, Godley and Fouilhoux, architects. *courtesy of the author*

 STEEL, BUILDING NO. 10

 STEEL ERECTION

 BUILDING NO. 10   FEBRUARY,

 STEEL WORKERS

 TRUSSES, THEATER NO. 10

 BUILDING NO. 10   MARCH,

 TOPPING OUT, BUILDING NO. 10

 DETAIL OF TOP

 GENERAL VIEW   MAY,

Progress photographs of the construction. Architects: Reinhard and Hofmeister; Corbett, Harrison and Mac Murray; Hood and Fouilhoux.   *courtesy of the author*

In this they were successful, immediately in one case and eventually in the other. The first, on the south corner, was acquired in 1930, but unfortunately the operators of the bar and tavern therein had a lease running until 1942 and nothing would induce them to surrender it. The new building went up around them, minus the corner, a piece about twenty feet by sixty-three. When 1942 came, it was hardly worthwhile to demolish the little corner building and replace it with such an expensive operation as an existing office building. Daniel Hurly and Patrick Daly continued as tenants on the old stand, this time over the barrel themselves, we may assume, as to the terms of the lease.

The north corner on 50th Street, a two story drug store, was finally acquired in 1970. Again there is a ground lease and it does not expire until 1983. Although allowance was made in the original plan for filling in the notches in the corner of RCA Building West, it looks as if they are there for some time to come.

Towards the center of the block, as demolition progressed, one speakeasy in an old brownstone refused to move. Everything tumbled down around it until it remained isolated like a tombstone, but still the tenant refused all inducement to move. Then one of the lawyers had a psychological idea. Policemen were retained to keep a twenty-four hour vigil on all sides of the building. Whenever the owner looked out a front window he saw policemen; whenever he looked out a back window he saw policemen. So what? That night he went to bed as usual. In the morning he took another look; the police were still there. They were there all day and still there when he went to bed that night. For some reason, however, he couldn't sleep and, for whatever reason that may have troubled him, he decided to leave, all on his own. He never came back. The next day the house came down in a cloud of brick dust and old plaster.

The first building to be completed was the RKO including the Music Hall. The grand opening of the latter was held on the rainy night of December 27th, 1932. As one of the newspapers, whose name is lost from my clipping, said:

> "In the grand foyer of the theater, where silver mirrors in panels four stories high, reflected and magnified the gleam of jewels and the rich shades of a thousand evening frocks, the shock brigade of newspaper photographers, with electric bulbs flashing bright over their heads, stemming the advancing tide again and again to beseech celebrities to stand and deliver just one smile into the pointed lenses."

For this great occasion there was not an act or a tripper that Roxy did not try to resurrect. What started as a gala occasion was by midnight a tedious drawn out affair. Even Roxy was worn out and the next day summoned his "wise men" to perfect the show. As one reporter commented:

> "Much of it seemed to this member of the six thousand sadly second rate stuff, out of place amid such triumphs of architecture and mechanics. Probably Roxy knows best, however."

Although the center of the new culture was off to a bad start, by the time it was opened up to the general public, Roxy's wise men had indeed been able to perfect the show. On through the depression and for long years thereafter the public were to queue up in the streets waiting to get into the popular shows.

The Center Theater opened more quietly a few days later. Curiously enough its patronage came from visitors outside the city and no effort was made to make it a competitor of the Music Hall. The Publicity Department put up their posters, not in the subways of New York, but on the billboards of Cincinnati, Louisville and Detroit. They saw to it that when a Mr. and Mrs. Harry Jones of South Honey Dew Lane in Topeka, Kansas made a trip to New York, it was a news item in the local social column, not failing to mention that the great event of their trip was their reservation of seats at the Ice-Capades at the Center Theater. It became the place to go in New York for Mr. and Mrs. Middle America. Still, the Center Theater never achieved the success of the Music Hall, and its program went through many changes. After some twenty years, it was torn down to make way for a better paying commercial venture, the addition of 1955 to the U.S. Rubber Building, now the Uniroyal.

During the next nine months the rest of the buildings of the first stage were completed, ending with the French Building in October, 1933. With the completion of the working drawings for these first buildings, most of the office force, including the writer, was let go to join the apple sellers on the street corners. With no better place to go I went back to the office of Raymond Hood on 40th Street, even though it was now just a place to hang my hat. Times had changed.

The Test of Time

Some forty years have gone by since Rockefeller Center outlived the dire prediction of its early critics, surviving the Depression as well, to become the great commercial and architectural success of its time. It has won a place in the hearts of the people of New York as a place to go on a Sunday walk, and has become the great attraction for out-of-town visitors. In June,

1969 it received the first twenty-five year Award of The American Institute of Architects "to recognize a distinguished design after a period of time has elapsed in which the function, esthetic statement, and execution can be reassessed." Rockefeller Center is not only a monument to the courage and perseverance of its promoters but to their foresight as well.

Today we would call the project one of "Urban Renewal." As a run down neighborhood replaced with something viable it was indeed all of that, carrying that part of the city along with it to a period of new growth and prosperity. Sixth Avenue became the Avenue of the Americas, a new face and a new image. Rockefeller Center has made a great contribution to the art of city planning and proved a stimulating example to the many kindred enterprises that have followed.

The original gridiron pattern of New York streets had been based on the multiple of residential size plots to make up the blocks and the streets were laid out to favor crosstown traffic from waterfront to waterfront. At that time the planners could not foresee the limitations the relatively narrow blocks would offer to the demands of future large scale buildings and enterprises. While the architects of Rockefeller Center were not successful in persuading the city to vary the street pattern in any schemes where they may have wished to do so, or even to bridge the streets, their development of three blocks as one unified scheme did awaken the city fathers to the importance of permitting variances of the rigid street patterns in the future. In this sense the three block development of Rockefeller Center opened the door to the superblock development in housing when interior streets were modified or closed in the interests of an overall plan.

Rockefeller Center began with the locating of the Opera, not as another building in a typical city block, but as the center of a three block development facing on a great public square. Unity of the three blocks, as far as pedestrian traffic was concerned, was achieved with the creation of the Concourse level below the streets, which was enlivened with shops and restaurants. The continuing influence of this concept may be seen in such projects as Place Marie in Montreal and Penn Center in Philadelphia. In Rockefeller Center the Concourse has since been extended across the Avenue of the Americas to include the new buildings on the west side of the Avenue as well as two buildings to the north.

The "Metropolitan Square" idea anticipated the advantage of integrating the site for an Opera with one for business. This developed into a little city of office space and entertainment with related services. Today we see the combination of day and night life, business and pleasure, activities of weekdays and weekends, as one of the basic reasons why the Center has so much vitality, successfully carrying on through good times and bad.

165

Rockefeller Plaza and Fountain.
courtesy of Impact Photos, Inc.

"Channel Gardens" Promenade leading to the Plaza.
courtesy of Jay Hoops

The idea of open space for people beyond that provided by the streets and sidewalks has characterized Rockefeller Center. Rockefeller Plaza and the esplanade to Fifth Avenue are enjoyed by every visitor to the Center who finds this one of the delights of a visit to New York, and this idea kept on growing as in the open ground area of the Lever Bros. Building and the Seagram Building on Park Avenue. On the west side of the Avenue of the Americas four new buildings have not only continued the idea of a concourse below grade, but of open space at ground level; although the amount of rental space above grade is of greater density per acre than the original Rockefeller Center, the proportion of ground given over to plazas, promenades, fountain and planting is far greater, more than forty percent.

Not only an important step in the design of new buildings of the time the provision for off-street loading was a type of improvement that was to become a requirement of the city in the future. If we seemed to have poked fun at Joe Brown with his concept of an automatic garage, perhaps now we can acknowledge his foresight too, for eventually a six story garage was built in the Center with a capacity for eight hundred cars as the lower part of the Eastern Airlines Building. This was another example of a commercial enterprise anticipating the trend towards more complete service within itself, and at the same time helping to get cars off the street.

Forty years is a long time in the life of a building, and there is a practical aspect to the continued success of Rockefeller Center: the older buildings of the Center have been constantly upgraded and never allowed to become obsolete. Perhaps such efforts began with trying to raise the "Graybar standard" at the very beginning. At any rate, today Rockefeller Center's standards of office space are the standard others strive to meet, and with it it maintains its class of tenants on which so much of its success depends. An example of the upgrading is air conditioning; when this became a standard feature of newer office space, Rockefeller Center was air conditioned, costly as it was to do afterward.

Even with the old critics a change of tune was noticed, and to the newer ones, it was the city that had to change to keep up with Rockefeller Center. Ten years later, the same Lewis Mumford said:

"What makes the Center architecturally the most exciting mass of buildings in the city is the nearby view of the play of mass against mass, of low structures against high ones, of the blank walls of the theaters against the vast checkerboard slabs of glass in the new garages. . . . Rockefeller Center has turned into an impressive collection of structures."

(Left) Final model for the RCA Building.
courtesy of the author

(Above) Study model of final scheme for Metropolitan Square, Sept. 1931
courtesy of author

(Opposite page) RCA Building nearing completion *courtesy of Samuel H. Gottscho*

Writing in the 1940's Mr. Frederick Lewis Allen said:

"There is something more to Rockefeller Center than the costly magnificence of sheer size. There is the use of light and color, and foliage, and fountains, and terraced construction, and clean orderly design to delight the eye. . . . It is clear that people enjoy the gayety of the cafe scenes below. I recall sitting one afternoon in the restaurant on the British side of the Plaza and looking out on the people strolling by, the bright yellow-green and blue-green umbrellas, the silver water coming down over the fountain steps below Prometheus, and beyond, the shadowed rear wall of the Time and Life Building; I tried to think what the scene reminded me of, and realized that it was a shipboard scene, full of animation and sunlight and the sense of holiday."

The architect I.M. Pei in his 1970 article on "Open Space" says that "The Rockefeller Center Plaza . . . is perhaps the most successful open space in the United States, perhaps in the world for that matter." Pei writes that it is a sequence of spaces, starting with the long and narrow "Channel Gardens" from Fifth Avenue to the Plaza ". . . spaces of two different proportions and two different aspects . . . much more interesting to walk through." In addition to "horizontal variety" it also has a "three dimensional variety; an up and down effect." Perhaps most significantly Pei continues:

"Spaces are for people. And people like to come to Rockefeller Center since this is a successful space. Now perhaps you will find more people in Wall Street per square foot, but I don't think you'll find the variety of people in Wall Street as you'll find right here in Rockefeller Center. People come here as tourists, they come here to shop, they come here to go to the theatres nearby. So we have the variety of activities right here, day as well as night. In their abstract sense, I would consider the Rockefeller Plaza far from ideal in terms of proportion. The spaces are perhaps a little to small for the size of the buildings that surround them. But in a way I'm glad that it isn't larger, because it creates a special kind of intensity here, because of this exaggerated proportion. Just as exaggeration is necessary for effect in theatre, so I think Rockefeller Center has succeeded in a way as good theatre."

"And how much," Raymond Hood had asked, "how much would it cost to recirculate 30,000 gallons of water a day?"

CHAPTER **VI**

BACK ON THE OLD STAND

The McGraw-Hill Building

The last of the skyscrapers designed in Raymond Hood's own office was the McGraw-Hill Building. Although work on the plan had started before I was transferred over to the Graybar Building for the Metropolitan Square project, I had little chance to work on it myself. Therefore the following is not a first hand report.

Earlier, the McGraw-Hill Co., publishers of technical books and journals, had occupied the Hill Building on Tenth Avenue and 36th Street since the merger of the two companies in 1916 following the death of Mr. John A. Hill. In the intervening years the new company had acquired several more publications and continued to expand. No longer under the one roof, something the president, James H. McGraw, considered important, the time had come to find a new location.

The first mention of moving came up in June 1929, a building committee was appointed in October and the site, some 47,000 sq. feet on West 42nd Street between Eighth and Ninth Avenues was acquired in May, 1930. Raymond Hood, now well recognized for the design of business buildings, was selected as the architect and Starret Bros. and Eiken as the builder. Although the "crash" of the Stock Market in October 1929 caused a halt in the project, Mr. McGraw was certain the setback in the market would be of short duration and quickly resumed speed with his project. Ground was broken in August of 1930 and the company moved into the new building in

October of 1931 with the intent of occupying about eighty percent of the building and leasing the rest. McGraw's optimism about the significance of the crash of 1929 proved to be a delusion. In 1930 the Great Depression really closed in, and the company, like everyone else faced difficult times. Harold W. McGraw, Jr., president of the company at this writing, was a boy of thirteen at the time. He recalls that the vast extent of empty floor space was a wonderful place to go roller-skating.

The site was a little far west of the general midtown business activities, but was selected by McGraw for its location between the two main post offices as well as Grand Central and Pennsylvania Stations. It was one of McGraw's sayings, "It's better for an editor to wear out the soles of his shoes than the seat of his pants." Travel was still by train.

Coming north as far as 42nd Street brought McGraw closer to the engineering societies, particularly the Engineers Club on West 40th Street, where his large acquaintanceships helped to keep him abreast of the times in the engineering world. The zoning law, incidentally, did not permit printing plants between Third and Seventh Avenues. The isolated location, as far as tall buildings were concerned, meant the new structure would dominate its part of the skyline for long years to come.

For the architect, the program of requirements called for the housing of all the activities of a large publishing company: composition, photoengraving, printing, binding, mailing, shipping, business and editing. For this reason the lower floors were designed for factory use, braced and reinforced to stand the weight and vibration of presses. The upper floors were designed to provide open areas for the large clerical staff. Loading platform and off-street docking for trucks were included on 39th Street for the shipping departments. In brief, it was a loft type building with a somewhat better interior finish. Within the zoning envelope, and meeting the space requirements of approximately 567,000 square feet, the outlines of the structure resulted in a building thirty-four stories high.

According to Raymond Hood, "Economy, efficiency and good working conditions were the three thoughts uppermost in mind when we first started plans for the McGraw-Hill Building. . . . The dimensions of the property led us to place floors in large units extending from street to street. In order to insure the maximum amount of natural light and ventilation, we provided the greatest window area possible." The elevators were centered so as to give the maximum lighted space all around. The exterior was an expression of these requirements.

The *New Yorker* wondered what expression the "Raymond Hood who delights in experimentation" was to find for this strictly business type building. It was the use of two elements of architectural design that prob-

172

(Opposite page) Dominating the skyline, the McGraw-Hill Building by Hood and Fouilhoux.   *courtesy of McGraw-Hill*

ably weren't even mentioned in his Beaux Arts days—sunlight and color.

To flood the space with sunlight from wherever the sun might be in the sky the windows extended from desk height to as near the twelve foot ceiling as the building code permitted and across all the space from column to column. This resulted in horizontal bands of windows. It was already customary to express skyscrapers vertically, of which there was no finer example than Hood's own *Daily News* Building, but now the horizontal bands of windows were accentuated in that direction rather than architecturally treated to express verticality. The masonry between the windows at the floor line was left in simple unbroken horizontal bands, and even the steel faced columns were slightly recessed to avoid any vertical accent. The McGraw-Hill became the "first skyscraper to emphasize the horizontal line."

This is the architects version of how the color was decided upon:

> "When we came to painting the building, we did not start out at the beginning to have blue, but tried different colors, such as yellow, orange, green, gray, red and even Chinese red, before we finally decided on the present coloring of Dutch blue at the base, with sea green window bands, the blue gradually shading off to a lighter tone the higher the building got, until, it finally blends off into the azure of the sky. . . ."

A somewhat different version is told by Roger Burlingame in his story of McGraw-Hill, *Endless Frontiers*. According to him the client, James McGraw, was a serious man and one not to be trifled with, and according to Burlingame the selection was made by McGraw himself:

> "At a meeting at which the architect submitted samples of colored terra-cotta, McGraw, over other objections insisted on green. Others wanted black with orange trim. But the chief was emphatic. He made a speech in favor of the green. He talked down the orange and black because his sons were Princeton enthusiasts and he said 'There's too much Princeton around here!' He even cited his Irish ancestry as a reason for his choice.
>
> "A year later when the building was half up, he saw it from his Tenth Avenue office. He had been away in the meantime in California. He was standing, as he looked out of the window with one of the people who had wanted black with orange trim. He pointed to the green terra cotta and said "Who picked that color?"
>
> His associate was amazed.
>
> "Why you did! I was there. Don't you remember, I was for black, but you convinced me so I voted as you did."
>
> "But it's not the green we picked."
>
> They went out and held the sample against the terra-cotta. "It's awful," said McGraw. "Perfectly awful. I must have been sick that day."

174

It's true times had changed since, McGraw wasn't well, and the Depression had now become something that would spoil anybody's outlook on life. It happens that, elsewhere in his story, Burlingame says McGraw had the trait of adopting others' ideas as his own, "a habit not uncommon among high executives." It may well have been that the architect and his client had had a meeting on the subject of the color of the building and Raymond Hood had been so successful in convincing McGraw it should be a blue green that the idea had become McGraw's own when the subject came up with his staff. And McGraw did eventually come to like the building as it was; before long everyone referred to it as "the green building."

For the exterior design of a large building to depend on color alone for its effect instead of the conventional architectural detailing in patterns, reveals and ornamentation was most unusual, but so was the use of plain smooth blocks of terra-cotta. While terra-cotta, a baked clay product, in this case with a glazed finish, is one of the oldest and most enduring of man-made building materials, its tendency to warp and twist in the baking process when used in large blocks had made its use for smooth walls impractical. Now a way had been found to add an aggregate of ground up terra-cotta biscuit to the wet clay, which minimized its tendency to change shape when being fired. Blocks large enough to use in Raymond Hood's scheme for the exterior were not unreasonable.

However, the glazed terra-cotta blocks had another characteristic that might well have limited their use in such an extent of plain surfaces in any case. While every precaution might be taken to mix the proportion of the color glazing uniformly, again, under the intense heat of the firing, finished products might exhibit little uniformity in the exact shade and tone of the color intended. For this job the manufacturing was a machine process and the economics of the usage of the large blocks depended on using "the run of the mill." The McGraw-Hill Building was the largest application of the of the process that had ever been tried and the manufacturer could not afford, at the price, to grade, select or cull the finished product.

If the chance were taken to place them in the wall as they came from the kiln to the job, a section of dark blocks from one load might be next to a batch of light ones from the next, giving a blotchy effect to the wall. The same thing might happen with the color tone, some being more greenish, others bluish. The burden of what to do to give a pleasing texture to the wall surface fell on the architect. After all, it was his idea in the first place. Somehow, the blocks would have to be selected and graded at the site at no cost to the owner.

In the office at this time was a young designer, Bob Carson, who was also an accomplished artist with a fine sense of color. When the time came to lay the terra-cotta blocks, he was set up in an office window across the street

175

Two views of the McGraw-Hill Building from 42nd Street looking west.

courtesy of Gottscho-Schleisner, Inc.

courtesy of McGraw-Hill

176

from the building. Before each block was laid it would be faced in his direction. Through a set of prearranged signals with the masonry foreman he would indicate where, along the walls, it should be laid to avoid disturbing contrasts, and thus he achieved a pleasing texture by proper distribution of the varied blocks.

A building that was striped the wrong way and lacked the conventional architectural detailing was not received without comment, particularly one that stood up on the skyline all by itself. The *New Yorker* called it "a stunt and not a successful one," and continued:

> "This type of design, which so many of our avant garde have borrowed from Germany, can always be counted on to start an architectural argument and for our part, we are by no means converted to it yet. A building may be, as the proponents of the horizontal line point out, merely a series of superposed floors, but the fact remains that a tall building considered as a mass, goes up, not sidewise."

To the *New Yorker,* the *Daily News* Building with its strongly vertical effect was "the finest in New York."

It is doubtful, though, whether the McGraw-Hill Building was accepted by the avant garde as a reflection of the European trend; the glass did not run around the corner to give the see-through effect of the modern buildings with their cantilevered corners. The McGraw-Hill Building had good steel columns in the corners, painted black at that. As for Hood, he was always too busy doing things as he saw them to pay much attention to what the avant garde or other philosophers of architecture thought about how things should be done.

The design in horizontal bands seemed to many people to create the optical illusion that the building leaned outwards as it went up. The architect and teacher of design, Burnham Hoyt, analyzed the cause of this: there are great rows of double hung windows, a type in which the upper sash slides outside the lower sash, the upper sash creating a small shadowline where it overhangs the lower. With no vertical accent in the architectural details, as is usual in tall buildings, the unrelieved repetition of the series of horizontal shadows of overhanging sash creates the illusion the building leans outwards.

Only a little more receptive was Arthur T. North, editor of the small volume of Raymond Hood's work:

> "Personally, I do find the building very interesting, not unattractive, and worthy of careful analysis. It is undoubtedly a decided step in a direction we cannot clearly distinguish at this time—and probably it cannot be worse architecture than many buildings we have endured in the past. . . . I have never seen anything like it."

177

North's question was in the title of his article: "But . . . Is It Architecture?

The Great Depression had meant the end of a great period in the development of the skyscraper and one that was epitomized by the work of Raymond Hood more than any other architect. The McGraw-Hill Building, with its departure from the accepted idea of what the lines of a skyscraper should be proved to be clearly in the direction that architecture would take in a new era. But before that new era was recognized, the Depression had to run its course and then another world war. Then came a new point of view, different purposes and a change in social outlook.

Writing in the *New York Times* in 1953, Lewis Mumford said of the McGraw-Hill Building:

> "The green tiled skyscraper was the first to discard vertical emphasis for horizontal bands of windows. More light and more flexibility of arrangement of interior space. Many of the post-war buildings followed this example.
>
> "While New York lagged behind Chicago in the development of the skyscraper, it had the ironic task in the thirties of bringing that form to its logical end: the Empire State Building for its actual height, the Daily News for its proud verticality, the McGraw-Hill Building for its horizontal bands of windows, and the New York Hospital for its spacious setting."

Further recognition of the work of Raymond Hood in American architecture was noted in *Cue* for June 1955, in a column by Emory Lewis on the "Everyday Face of New York:"

> "Many architects of New York office buildings have come up with the simple solution of placing ever smaller boxes on larger ones to achieve a sense of solidity of space. . . . Most of them have followed the pioneering McGraw-Hill Building (1931) and discarded vertical emphasis for horizontal bands of windows. Sunlight in the offices has won a battle 1935–55. These buildings are an enormous improvement over the self conscious turrets and spires of yesterday. There is, however, a sameness about them. In the struggle against yesterdays rococo, individuality has been lost."

At least, as the pioneer, Raymond Hood held his place as an individual.

Crackers and Soup

The McGraw-Hill Building was done now, and so was the work on Capt. Patterson's residence, and the World's Fair. Nothing more was coming in. The drafting room was quiet, the boards vacant—no calls from jobs under construction, no voice of Mr. Campbell, the old chief draftsman, "Listen, we're in a tight situation at the Nurses' Home."

The Crash had come and gone. This was the Great Depression, and the one or two of us still around, exclusive of the accountant and two secretaries, were welcome to come in out of the rain but we had to find our own work. One man, Don Hatch, did have a job for Raymond Hood, working on a housing scheme for the poor. The New Deal was under way, and for architects it was survival work, each project shared by two or three firms. Faced with no work at all, architects, like many other people, began to have a little appreciation and sympathy for the life of people who had always gone without.

Yet in the end, despite all the high ideals expressed, housing for the poor at a rent they could afford to pay was never achieved. Somebody higher up the economic ladder always moved into the new buildings and the poor got the leftovers. Although for many of the architects, housing was a starvation job, many others began to feel that architects, too, had a social obligation

Housing Project during the depression by Raymond Hood, one of a group of architects.

courtesy of the author

to their fellow man. To these, the old saying "the wise man buildeth the house of the wicked" was not enough. But the new collective client had little idea of what an architect was or what he could do to improve life in the city of the future. Even in the office there was little discussion of such philosophy at this time, for at lunch time we all chipped in for a can or two of Campbell's soup and a box of Uneeda Biscuits, with perhaps a symbolic apple from the nearest street corner for dessert. The Depression was real in every detail. Raymond Hood played little part in this. For one thing, he was not well and was seen less and less at the office.

"By God, I Am"

Hood's illness lasted about a year. He had a period of recovery and then the trouble came back. Still, after a stay at the Fifth Avenue Hospital it began to look as if he was on his feet once more. Then came a terrible blow for Hood. It was in the days of the Lindbergh tragedy, and like many others, Hood received a letter threatening to kidnap his children if a large sum of money were not paid at once. Hood was threatened with having acid thrown in his face. Consulting certain special police, Hood was advised to send his family out of the country immediately, and if he could not go with them he, too, should stay elsewhere and not return to his house.

Hood's wife took the children to Bermuda, and he stayed with an old friend and neighbor Ray Morris at the Morris' house. Morris had given him one of his first jobs, the new house at the time of their marriage. Before long, Hood was able to join his own family in Bermuda, and once more seemed in good health. Mrs. Hood wrote back to Don Hatch at the office that Hood "had a good trip down and (was) taking it good and easy. . . . Saw the doctor this morning and I am sure he is going to do Raymond a lot of good—in that he thinks he needs letting alone for a couple of weeks."

Don Hatch was working on plans for alterations to Hood's house in Stamford and was corresponding with Mrs. Hood about it. Despite the optimism of the above letter, it was soon clear that things were not going well with Hood himself; aside from directions about the house, in her letter of February nineteenth Mrs. Hood writes that "Mr. Hood hasn't been feeling at all well since last Thursday . . . I don't know whether it's the reaction from those injections or what."

The Hoods returned to their house in Stamford, for the perpetrator of the threat had been caught, a young student thinking of an easy way to raise money. At random the culprit had checked off names of prominent professional people, with no knowledge at all of his victims or their circumstances and with no plan to carry out his threat.

Last portrait photograph of
Raymond Hood.
    courtesy of Hood family

As an indication of the emotional strain Hood had been under, he collapsed on learning of the student's capture. At some time during this last year, Caleb Hornbostel came to New York and stopped in to see Hood. It was already late in the day and the sky over the city was darkening and the lights were coming on. Caleb, the son of Hood's old employer in Pittsburgh, was now himself an architect. Recalling the old days in Pittsburgh, Caleb reminded Hood of his parting words as he left the old office to seek his fortune in New York, "to become the greatest architect in New York."

Raymond Hood smiled and took Caleb over to the window. The roofs were still low between the American Radiator Building and Rockefeller Center. Over the line of roofs loomed the great mass of the RCA Building, silhouetted against the skyglow of the city. Within its fabric, too, shone the lights of countless windows. It was Raymond Hood's favorite view of Radio City and his favorite time of day. "To become the greatest architect in New York, you say? Well," he said, pointing to the RCA Building, "by God, I am."

181

Raymond Hood died of rheumatoid arthritis on August 15th, 1934. His old friend Westbrook Pegler wrote in the World-Telegram:

> "He was a modest little fellow, not much larger than a jockey but he did enjoy his success as an architect, and he must have acknowledged to himself, he was somebody, although he never was to admit as much to anybody else."

> "He had tackled the biggest, toughest town in the world, where the competition is the hardest, alone, broke and handicapped by personal shyness. Before he died, two weeks ago, he had shown the whole world."

"Whatsoever Thy Hand Findeth"

At the start of his career, when Hood moved to his new office in the American Radiator Building, a little beaten-up pocket edition of a King James Bible turned up. On the fly-leaf in a strong bold hand was written "Whatsoever thou puttest thy hand to do, do with all thy might." It was signed, "Mother."

Raymond Hood was fortunate that he chose architecture as his profession by the time he was ready for M.I.T. As he wrote from Paris a little later, "My method of progress is no more precise than this—to do everything that comes up as thoroughly as possible and not miss an opportunity—to work blindly but hard." The precepts of his mother were to start Hood on his way, yet with characteristic insight he noted that "in New York one easily falls into the habit of working without thinking on account of the amount of work there is to do." The value of his stay in Paris, he felt, was in having time to think, and "to order his life."

In any case, hard work was a habit by the time Hood became a family man, and according to Mrs. Hood, after failing to come home one night, his excuse when he finally appeared was that he had been so exhausted from working late that he fell asleep on the office couch. "Of course I had to believe him."

A willingness to work hard does not assure success, and in Hood's case, opportunity was a long time in coming to his door. When it did, it was to tap the shoulder of a man of small stature, and a shy nature. The might he would apply was not to be in physical stature, arrogance, or the will to dominate others. His was another gift. George Pauley, one of the first in Hood's new office, told me of a trip he made with Hood, who had been asked to design an office building for one of the southern cities. Because the site appeared to be large enough, Hood thought the office building would be quieter, have better light, and more circulation of air if he could set it

(*Opposite page*) Rockefeller Center at Night   *courtesy of Samuel H. Gottscho*

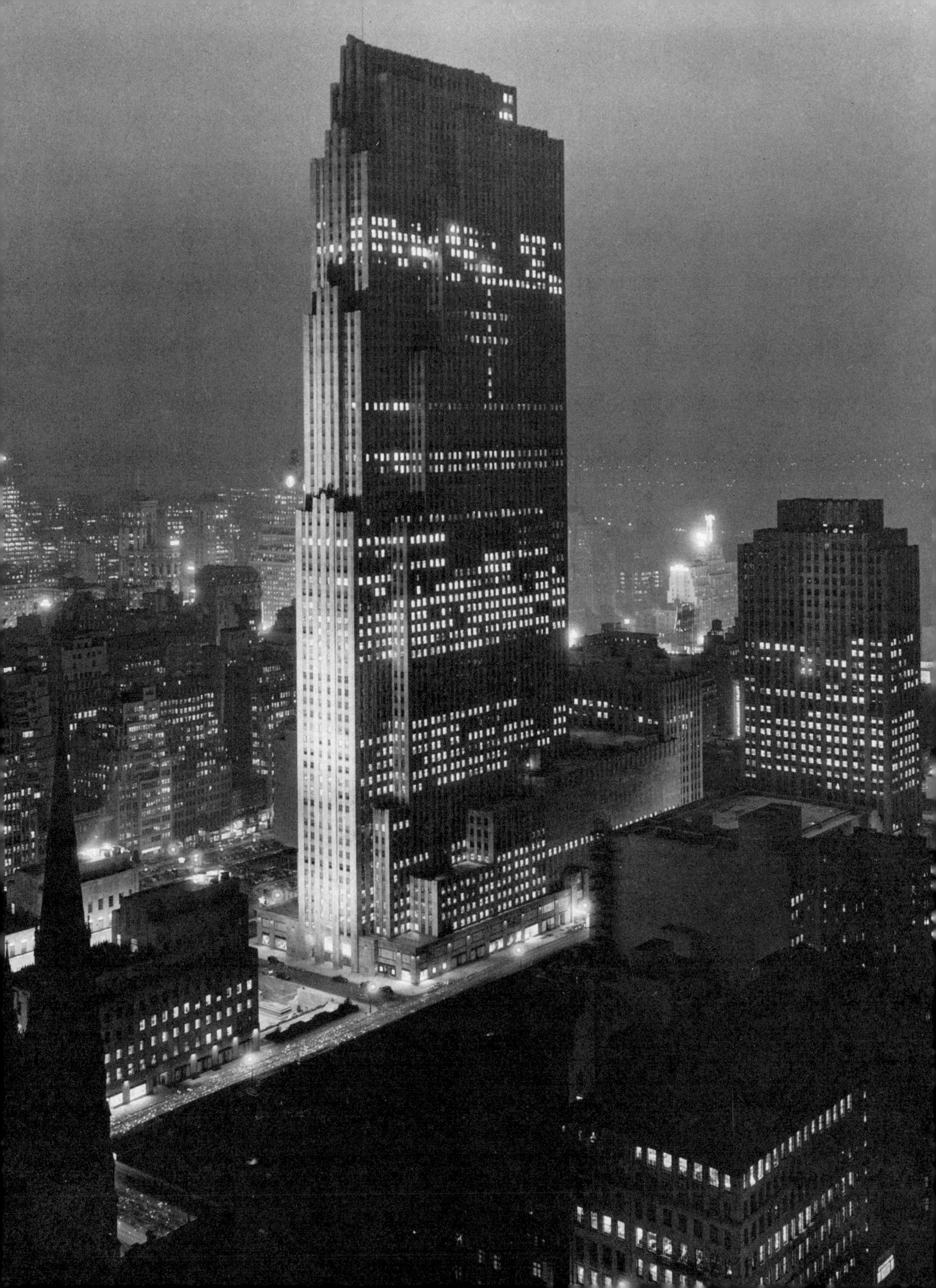

back from the street. He worked out a very interesting scheme and when it was done, he and George took it to a meeting of the owners and their real estate advisors.

Hood's drawings were put up on an easel in the front of the room, and then the local real estate people proceeded to tear them to pieces. They had a distinguished New York architect down there who thought he knew something about office buildings, so they were out to show him that he didn't know much. Here he had been given an expensive lot on the main street of town, and what did he do with it? Design a building where most of it was as far away from the street as possible. "Everybody knows," said the real estate men, "that it's the offices on the main street that get the high rental, and this building is all back."

According to George, it was a very hot day and Hood had taken off his coat and was unconcernedly walking up and down in back of the room, smoking a cigar. Finally the local people finished their criticisms and said, "Well, Mr. Architect, what have you got to say now?"

Unruffled, Hood went up to the front of the room. "Well," he began, "this has been very interesting. I realize those of us who come from the big cities think we know all there is to know and it has been a great privilege to come down here and find out that there are other ways of looking at things. But you know, speaking about this building being all back, we just finished a big office building in Chicago. Strange as it may seem, all the suites on the back of that building were rented immediately, and to this day there are vacant ones on North Michigan Avenue."

The local people thought this over and, becoming rather more amenable, finally decided they liked the plan the way it was. It was not until George and Hood were on the way back on the train that Hood suddenly burst out laughing and laughed so hard that George nearly had to hold him in his seat. When he had calmed down, George asked him what was so funny.

"Well, you know, there wasn't a soul in that room that realized that the back of the Chicago Tribune Building is on Lake Michigan."

Hood's solution may have been guileful, but it showed that he had a talent for turning the tide with a touch of mischief. No matter what the provocation, he never let his hackles rise. His strength in putting his ideas across was found in the parable, the apt story, and the humorous parallel. With perspicacity and insight, Hood went into any fight for his ideas confident that he would have the right word at the right time. No matter how tough the struggle, even the burliest client would lose without realizing he had never had a chance to fight.

Still, Hood sometimes met his master at the same game, like Capt. Patterson who had his own sense of humor. Even John R. Todd admired Hood for his ideas, once conceding that Raymond Hood would always come to meetings all fired up with ideas, perhaps twenty, of which nineteen would be all wet but there was always one good one.

Ray Hood's enthusiasm for what he was doing was infectious for student and businessman alike. To the client a miserable commercial job became part of a bigger game and far more worthwhile. As Tallmadge said, "Hood was a flame of vigor, imagination and daring. His enthusiasm and eloquence coaxed clients along paths they never would have trodden in their saner moments." This was Hood's strength and gift in the lion's den.

As those of us who were with Hood knew, this took a tremendous drain of emotional and mental energy when the going was hard, yet Hood never lost his sense of humor. Again as Tallmadge said, "His life was a joy ride in which everybody got a thrill, including the client."

All of this triumph of will would have been a hollow victory if Hood did not, indeed have something to put over. First of all was Hood's love of designing the building for its own sake, as well as that of the client. As he once said of the typical business building, "For the client it is a chance to get a return on his money, for the manufacturer a chance to sell his products, for the contractor a chance to make a profit. There remains the architect, the building's only friend."

If Raymond Hood was a leading figure of his period it may well be asked what were the theories he believed in and what was his philosophy of architecture? From the point of view of the critic or historian I don't think Raymond Hood had any philosophy of architecture in the intellectual sense. One can search through his work in vain to prove him an exponent of the coming International style. Hood was a doer, not a theorist. Unlike Le Corbusier his lessons were taught through his buildings, not his writings. He was not concerned with the social significance of architecture as were the Europeans. As Walter L. Creese wrote to me in 1958,

> "It seems to me that Hood's work should be understood within the context of the American situation at his time. The bigness, the speed, the frustrations of American practice at that period appear to have given his work a particular character. At the same time he was a man with a remarkable number of pertinent and original ideas, and I think as you told me once, very cognizant of European theory at the time. My main point would be, therefore, that if you try to measure him against advanced European theory of the time that American intellectuals will say, 'Well, his theories were not as advanced as those of contemporary Europe.' This is partially true. However, on the other hand, he did accomplish a great

deal and I always have the sense that American accomplishment must be measured against the fact that ideas and theories are not as easily accepted, or were not in his time, as they are in Europe. This is a kind of endurance lesson from my point of view."

One of the first to recognize Raymond Hood as the great skyscraper architect was Prof. John Kouwenhoven in 1948. Writing in his book, *Made In America,* Kouwenhoven develops his theory that Hood was the greatest of the vernacular architects as well:

"What we need to know, and someday may know when Hood's life is properly written, is what he meant when he said, late in life, to Kenneth Murchison, 'This beauty stuff is all bunk.' "

"On the evidence of Hood's two greatest buildings it seems safe to assume that he meant something very like what the Shaker elder, Frederick Evans, had meant back in the 1870's when he told Charles Nordhoff that Shaker buildings ignored 'architectural effect and beauty of design' because what people called 'beautiful' was 'absurd and abnormal.' Like the Shakers, the designer of the McGraw-Hill Building had an eye to more light, a more equal distribution of heat, and a more general care for protection and comfort. But no beauty, if beauty was something apart from such things as these."

To dodge the challenge and pick up the reference of Prof. Kouwenhoven as to what Hood meant when he said "This beauty stuff is all bunk" we may find the answer in an article written by Hood in the issue of *Liberty Magazine* for December 7th, 1929, entitled, "What is Beauty in Architecture?" It would seem to confirm Prof. Kouwenhoven's observations:

"I cannot tell what beauty is, but I can tell what it is not. Beauty is not a gas, a thin liquid coating, or a perfume that, vaporized over an object, lifts it out of itself into a state of art but of diminished usefulness. It is not 'a touch of blue in just the right spot,' nor is it any other talismanic touch that transforms an ugly object into a thrilling masterpiece. If there is beauty at the end of such a process, it was surely there in large part at the beginning. . . ."

Further along Hood defines:

". . . a path to beauty that satisfies me—at least for the moment. It is that beauty is utility, developed in a manner to which the eye is accustomed by habit, insofar as this development does not detract from its quality of usefulness. Habit, tradition, and environment facilitate the recognition and acceptance of beauty. They form the sugar coating without which perverse human nature might at times reject even what it really likes. But the intellect and reason pronounce final judgment. If an object satisfies the intellect, it is immaterial whether or not it conforms to any theory of beauty, any system of composition, any accepted rule of art, or any philosophical analysis. It is beauty.

"Go back through all the periods of architecture, the styles of furniture and decoration, and the development of all the objects and implements that we use. Wherever a claim can be laid to having produced beauty, you will find that the one common factor is utility. . . .

"There is no mechanical contrivance or implement of pure utility developed to a degree of perfection that does not attract and hold the attention of even the purest aesthetes by its form and expression. Certainly the steam locomotive was produced with no conscious search for beauty, and it cannot be put aside with the trite explanation that it is an expression of power. . . ."

One of Hood's further examples was, "a beautiful woman! I contend that even her beauty is in proportion to her utility . . ." Summing up his theory, Hood writes:

"All of this is not proof, but evidence piles mountain-high to indicate that one of two things is true—utility produces beauty; or in some unknown way it weaves itself without the least conscious effort into the formation of most things that are beautiful.

"The search for beauty might be likened to Maeterlinck's allegory in "The Bluebird." Just as the two children went out into the wide world to search for the bluebird of happiness, and finally came back to find it in the garden they had left, so we leave all the common articles and conceptions of everyday life and wander forth looking for a sophisticated, mysterious something or other that will fulfill our idea. And then one day the path leads us back to the garden we had left—we find that all the simple things are beautiful and that there is no mysterious complications about it. Real beauty lies in usefulness. Does any other answer give us so much comfort and satisfaction?"

It sounds as if the writer of the above was the designer of the *Daily News* Building and not the Chicago Tribune with its Gothic tracery. Indeed, as we have already noted by the time of the News Building, Hood was ready to say, during a discussion of how to treat the outside, ". . . to decorate the exterior of a skyscraper is like trying to put a lace shawl on an elephant."

Hood was in the front line and not the ivory tower; his approach to architecture was simple. As far as he was concerned, the client was the boss, and as his architect it was up to him to find the best solution to his problem that he could and to work out the best way to carry it out. It was sufficient for Hood that he worked in a society to whom business was business. Big

187

business was concentrated in New York and Hood, too, had come to New York to help devise more efficient structures in which this concentration of business could do its work. But in the resulting skyline there was a contagious excitement felt by the man in the street as well as the architect.

Furthermore, according to Hood, if the client was the "boss" he should serve, the client also provided the opportunity to carry out bigger ideas. The *Daily News,* for Hood, was one little step toward his idea of the future city of skyscrapers. Hood did not see skyscrapers as promoting congestion; as Harvey Wiley Corbett said, "People swarm to the city because they like congestion." Hood felt "Congestion is good. It's the best thing we have in New York. The glory of the skyscraper is that we have provided for it so well." To Hood it was a triumph of New York that you could house in one city block as many business people as would have been spread over one square mile of Paris. Instead of clogging the streets with their comings and goings they communicated with each other by going up and down in elevators, all in the same building. Any one of many thousands of people could be within five minutes of your office if you wanted to see them. Where else in the world was anything like this possible?

All this made for better business. Hood would have liked to have gone further and improved the relation of a working man's home to his place of business. New York was already densely built up as far as the location of

Model of apartment scheme for country living.
courtesy of McGraw-Hill

Bridges of Skyscraper Apartments.
courtesy of Hugh Ferris

apartments near business centers was concerned. To alleviate this situation Hood came up with the idea of great bridges of skyscraper-apartments across the rivers, an idea seconded in Hugh Ferris' sketch for the same in his book *Metropolis of Tomorrow*. Raymond Hood carried the idea further to combining offices, apartments, stores, hotels and theaters in one great building covering three blocks, so that all activities of daily life could take place within one building, an idea which recalled his conglomerate idea for the "greatest cathedral in the world" the early project for Columbus, Ohio he was proposing to the Pastor when I first entered his office.

People were moving to the suburbs in increasing numbers, and Hood tackled the problem in a new way. According to the following account:

> "A tract of about 100 acres near Dobbs Ferry was to be split up into one and one-half or two-acre plots for a residential building development, and Hood was asked to draw plans for the group of one-family houses. After a while Hood turned in a plan for a ten-story building to occupy the tract, the many beautiful trees on the land left standing."

The *News Tribune* of Providence interviewed Hood about this project in January, 1932, and quoted him as follows:

> "Why not make it a tower? It fits everybody. The average family of city dwellers dislikes the coal bill, the repair bill, taxes and the countless expenses of running a detached house. He does like open country, trees, lakes and light and air. In a tower he has it all.
> "Why pull up all these beautiful trees, these elms of New England, cut up the countryside to form new 'real estate developments' as the city

189

spreads, build a network of gas and water mains, roads and sidewalks, wires and sewers? The city man lives outside the city because he likes the country. Why not give him the country as is? He can have his house in the tower where all the business of living is concentrated—yet with plenty of personal privacy, mind you—and the country at his very door, wild and unspoiled.

"Expense? Cheaper! Saves money for everybody. There's only one roof to pay for. Heat comes from one boiler water from a single main; is carried away in one sewer. Savings are made all along the line, and the tenant benefits directly. Can't you see the picture? Out in the open country where few men think they can ever afford to live? Where they'd move tomorrow if they could? Believe it or not, that's what we're coming to."

Hood's early appreciation of the importance of conserving the landscape in building development was indeed a look to the future when "Environmental Quality" was to become a household word.

Like historians, many architects are concerned with style in their buildings, following one historic precedent or another as fashion or demand dictates or even a contemporary mode, itself so soon to become a historic style as well. Prof. Bush-Brown, professor of Architectural History at M.I.T. wrote to me of Raymond Hood in 1958:

"It has always seemed to me that Hood's career was a tribute to a discipline previously undergone and that he remained free of any of the theoretical 'literary associations' attached to styles, so that he went after strong design without inhibiting misconceptions about what an architect should be doing. He never once, as far as I know, thought that Gothic was appropriate for an Anglican church, for example, or that a modernist had to be a social reformer. Some of his remarks about his facility in different styles may be interpreted as fits of irresponsible eclecticism, but that is erroneous, I believe, since, like all great architects, Hood struck first for a unified composition of masses and spaces, arranged for performance and monumentality; style was an incident, though he ultimately found himself working with greatest vigor in a style of his own day."

Hood was only fifty-three when he died, but in the brief time of ten years his work had bridged the era that saw the end of eclecticism and the coming of the International style in America—from the *Tribune* Tower to the McGraw-Hill Building. The era between those two buildings was the great age of the skyscraper, and of all the architects of the period he stands as its symbol. We can see this great transition and development take place through the works of this one man with his tremendous imagination, receptiveness and awareness of his times. His development and stature never ceased growing—and in different times, it would have seemed a tragedy that he did not live to carry out the promise of greater work in the days to come. As it was the Depression itself closed the door.

In making a posthumous award to Hood, the New York Chapter of the American Institute of Architects stated:

> "Hood was an inspiration to his students. Beyond his actual buildings, his imaginative projects of all sorts and kinds evidenced a vision of the architecture of the future, which marked him as an outstanding genius of his period.
> "The record of his important buildings demonstrates his great breadth of vision and willingness to change. Starting with the winning design for the Chicago Tribune, which in form and detail followed the then accepted Gothic tradition of skyscrapers, he ran the whole gamut through the News Building, the Chicago World's fair, Rockefeller Center and the McGraw-Hill Building."

Hood was not one to take the limelight in a collective enterprise and was the last to be unwilling to share the billing with the less talented. Writing in *Vanity Fair* in December, 1931 John Fistere well said of him:

> ". . . Raymond Hood, seemingly less of a genius than Mr. Wright, but perhaps more of an architect—is happier sticking to his last than he is in making speeches and giving interviews—Hood's most promising trait is his inconsistency—'I would never build the same building twice.' "

Hood's works are vital because each one expressed a new idea. To Hood the idea was only half the battle, in fact worthless if he did not see it carried out. It was in this spirit of the fight to the end that he showed his determination and courage.

To Ely Jacques Kahn, Hood's fellow architect and longtime companion of the "Four-Hour Lunch Club" at Mori's, "He was a modest, forceful, positive dreamer who brushed aside trifles and searched for the solution to the problem in hand—the more difficult the better."

Short as Hood's day was, he would have been the last to say his life lacked fulfillment. At the time, he himself said, "So the architects face the problems of a new and modern city, the problems which architects and city planners have dreamed for years. Can there, then, be a greater time and place for an architect?"

courtesy of Samuel H. Gottscho

BIBLIOGRAPHY

with Acknowledgments to Lois Eaton, John B. Schwartzman, Merrill Wilson Koppe.

1. GENERAL

Banham, Reyner	*Architecture of the Well-tempered Environment,* Univ. of Chicago Press, 1969
Burchard, John Ely & Bush-Brown Albert	*The Architecture of America,* Boston, Little, Brown, 1961
Edgell, George H.	*American Architecture of Today,* C. Scribner's Sons, 1928
Ferris, Hugh	*The Metropolis of Tomorrow,* Washburn Press, 1929
Ferris, Hugh	"Power in Buildings," Columbia U. Press, 1953
Giedion, Sigfried	*Space, Time & Architecture,* Oxford Univ. Press, 1941 Harvard U. Press, 1949
Hilberseimer, L.	*Contemporary Architecture,* Chicago, P. Theobold, 1964
Holden, Arthur	*Sonnets for My City,* Schulte Pub. Co., 1965
Jacobs, Jane	"Death and Life of Great American Cities" Random House, 1961, p. 181-182
Joedicke, Jurgen	*History of Modern Architecture,* New York, Praeger, 1960
Kimball, Fiske & Edgell, G. H.	*History of Architecture,* Harper & Bros., 1918
Kouwenhoven, John	*Made in America,* Doubleday, 1948
Kouwenhoven, John	*Architecture as Environmental Technology*
LeCorbusier	*Vers Une Architecture,* 1924
LeCorbusier	*Urbanisme,* 1927
Mujica, F.	*History of Skyscrapers,* 1928
Scully, Vincent	*Modern Architecture,* New York, G. Braziller, 1961
Sexton, R. W.	"The Logic of Modern Architecture," (Architectural Book Publishing Co., 1929)
Tallmadge, Thomas E.	*The Story of Architecture in America,* New York, W. W. Norton & Co., 1927
Tunnard, Christopher & Reed, Henry Hope	*American Skyline,* Boston, Houghton Mifflin, 1955

2. RAYMOND HOOD

North, Arthur Tappan	McGraw-Hill Book Co., 1931. *Contemporary American Architects,* Raymond M. Hood
Adams, Rayne	Raymond Hood, *Architecture,* Mar. 1931
Profile	"Man Against the Sky," *New Yorker,* 1931

3. PUBLISHED MATERIAL by Raymond Hood

The American Radiator Bldg. New York	*The American Architect,* Nov. 19, 1924
Exterior Design of Office Buildings	*The Architectural Forum,* Vol. 41, 1924
Business Executives Office	*Pencil Points,* March 1929
The Spirit of Modern Art	*The Architectural Forum,* Nov. 1929
Beauty in Architecture	*The Architectural Forum,* Nov. 1930
The News Building	*The Architectural Forum,* Nov. 1930
What is Beauty in Architecture	*Liberty,* Dec. 7, 1929
Hanging Gardens of New York	*N.Y. Times* Magazine, Aug. 23, 1931
The Design of Rockefeller Center	*The Architectural Forum,* Jan.-June. 1932
The Apartment House Loggia	*The Architectural Forum,* Jan. 1934

4. THESES

Creese, Walter L., Ph.D.	American Architecture 1918-33, Harvard
Kilham, Walter H., Jr.	On the Zoning Law of New York 1928, Harvard
Koppe, Miss Merrill Wilson	The Architecture of Raymond Hood, NYU
Schwartzman, John B.	Raymond Hood, The Unheralded Architect, Univ. of Virginia, 1962

5. CONTEMPORARIES mentioned in text

BUCHMAN and KAHN (ELY JACQUES)

> North, Arthur Tappan: *Contemporary American Architects* (1931 Whittlesey Pr.)
> American Architect: January 1926 op. 185ff. atd p. 307ff.
> Architectural Record: April 1928 p. 289ff.

CORBETT, HARVEY WILEY, FAIA

> American Architect: 1921 vol. 119 pp. 603-08, 617
> American Architect: February 29, 1926 plate 25
> Parnassus: vol. 1, April 1929 p. 6-7

HARMON, ARTHUR LOOMIS, FAIA

> Architecture: February 1923 p. 41ff
> Architectural Record: vol. 58 July 1925 p. 1ff. (Shelton Hotel)
> L'Architecte: Vol. 3, 1926 p. 14-83 (Shelton Hotel)

HOWELLS, JOHN MEAD, FAIA

> American Architect: December 1928 p. 787ff. (Pan-Hell.)
> Parnassus: vol. 1, 1929 p. 5-6 (Pan-Hall.)
> Architectural Record: June 1930 p. 782ff. by Howells "Vertical or Horizontal Design?")
> Who's Who in American Art? p. 1146 vol. 16, 1930-31.
> Book (with no publisher or publishing date in it—just photographs of his work) "John Mead Howells"

RIVERA, DIEGO

Wolf, Bertram D. "The Fabulous Life of Diego Rivera, Stein & Davis 1963
Born, Esther "The New Architecture of Mexico"

URBAN, JOSEPH

Architecture: May 1934 pp. 240-90
Architectural Record: April 1930 p. 388ff.
Architecture: May 1930 p. 278ff.

WALKER, RALPH, FAIA

Walker, Ralph Henahan House 1957

WRIGHT, FRANK LLOYD

An Autobiography of Frank Lloyd Wright, 1st Edition, Longmans Green

6. BUILDINGS

The Chicago Tribune	The Chicago Tribune Competition, 1922
The Tribune Tower	Architectural Record, March 1923
The News	
Leo E. McGivena	News Syndicate Co., 1969
The Beaux Arts Apartments	Architectural Forum, Sept. 1930
McGraw Hill	
Burlingame, Roger	Endless Frontiers, McGraw Hill

Rockefeller Center

Allen, Frederick Lewis	Radio City—Cultural Center, Harpers Magazine, April 1932
Allen, Frederick Lewis	"Look at Rockefeller Center" Harpers, Oct. 1938
Crowell, Merle	"The Story of Rockefeller Center," Arch. Forum, May 1932
Finance Committee Reports, Etc. as to renewals of Leases On The upper Estate	1888—Columbia Univ.
Haskel, Douglas	Roxy's Advantage over God, The Nation, 5 Jan. 1933
Haskel, Douglas	Frank Lloyd Wright and the Chicago Fair, The Nation, 3 Dec. 1930
Klein, Clare	The Rockefeller Center Property, C.V.Q., Feb. 1941
Loth, David	"City Within a City," Wm. Morrow & Co., 1966
Mumford, Lewis	"Radio City" Creative Arts, April 19, 1931
Rockefeller, John D., Jr.	The Founding of Rockefeller Center, 1961, The Last Rivet
Roxy	"How Radio City was Born," Variety, 20 Dec. 1932
Weisman, Winston	"Who Designed Rockefeller Center," Journal S.A.H., Vol. V No. 1, March 1951
Whitaker, Charles Harris	"Romeses to Rockefeller"

INDEX

1911   192